GW00724951

YOU SAY TOMATOES

by Bernard Slade

SAMUEL FRENCH, INC.
45 West 25th Street   NEW YORK 10010
7623 Sunset Boulevard HOLLYWOOD 90046
LONDON   TORONTO

2

IMPORTANT BILLING AND CREDIT REQUIREMENTS

YOU SAY TOMATOES by Bernard Slade was first produced on July 21st, 1994 at the Vineyard Playhouse in Vineyard Haven on Martha's Vineyard. The production was directed by Eileen Wilson and designed by Jim Haney with lighting by Ernest W. Iannaccone. The cast was as follows:

GILES ST. JAMES ------------------- Derek Murcott
FRED CRADDOCK ----------------- David Ponting
LIBBY DANIELS -------------------- Celia Howard
DAISY HOLIDAY --------------- Kristina Kreyling

CHARACTERS

(in order of appearance)

GILES ST. JAMES: Late fifties-early sixties, rumpled, eccentric, extremely private, stubborn, shy but quite articulate when necessary. English.

FRED CRADDOCK: An eminently likeable Londoner blessed with a natural wit and a cheerful attitude. His spry movements are those of a man much younger than his seventy years.

LIBBY DANIELS: A quintessential New Yorker about the same age as Giles. Only apparently confident, she is sometimes abrasive, but ultimately endearing.

DAISY HOLIDAY: A pretty woman in her twenties with an appealing, enthusiastic attitude towards life. Her distinctive Southern accent, along with her wide-eyed optimism, sometimes causes people to under-estimate her intelligence.

SETTING

The action of the play takes place over some three weeks in the living rooms of a cottage in Sussex and an apartment in the East Village of New York City.

The play is performed in two acts and six scenes.

YOU SAY TOMATOES

ACT

Scene 1

SCENE: *Late afternoon of a rainy autumn day in the present.*

The living room of a fairly isolated Seventeenth Century cottage a few miles outside a village in West Sussex. There is a front door that opens directly to the outside, another exit that leads to the unseen kitchen and some stairs that presumably lead to the upstairs bedrooms. The room is furnished with well-worn English country antiques, faded area rugs, comfortable chairs and a sofa, and is large enough to contain a table that can be used to serve meals. Although the place overflows with books and magazines and looks lived-in and undecorated, the room is reasonably tidy and warmly attractive. The low-beamed ceilings, fireplace, leaded pane windows, reinforce the nostalgic view of a quintessential, traditional, country English room.

AT RISE: *The STAGE is empty for a moment or two before GILES ST. JAMES enters from the kitchen carrying two perfect looking, large vegetable marrows which he places on the table, stands back and admires.*

HE has obviously just been working in the garden and is wearing a mud-splattered, somewhat damp jumper and Wellington boots. HE is in his late fifties or early sixties, rumpled, eccentric, often vague, extremely private, bright, stubborn, shy but articulate when necessary and not without a sense of humor. HE speaks with a regionally unaccented, pleasant voice. HE polishes one of the marrows with his elbow and then, as we hear a CRACK OF THUNDER, moves to look out the window.

As the RAIN starts to pour down, the front door is pushed open and FRED CRADDOCK, wearing a wet raincoat with his arms full of grocery bags, enters. An eminently likeable Londoner blessed with a natural, unforced, sly wit and a cheerful attitude, his spry movements are those of a man much younger than his seventy years.

They have known one another since Giles was a boy, and their relationship is more one of friendship than that of an employer and employee.

FRED. Give me a hand with these, will you? I don't want to get water on my nice, clean floor. (*As GILES crosses to him.*) Where'd all this mud come from then?

GILES. What? Oh, sorry, Fred—I was out in the garden. Didn't notice how hard it was raining. (*HE takes grocery bags from FRED.*)

FRED. Well, take your Wellie's off now, there's a good chap.

(GILES puts bags on table, peers into them as HE kicks off his Wellingtons, revealing that HE is wearing different colored socks, and FRED divests himself of his raincoat and wipes his shoes on the doormat.)

FRED. Looks like we're really going to catch "what for" tonight. Forecast on the radio said we could be in for a hurricane.

GILES. Then it'll probably be nice and sunny. When you were in town, did you notice the condition of the pitch?

FRED. Why would I do that?

GILES. We're playing Haslemere on Saturday. Last match of the season. Was it soggy?

FRED. *(Moves to table, proceeds to take items out of bags through following.)* I don't know, Giles. You know how I feel about cricket. I always need someone to tell me when they're actually playing.

GILES. That's because you don't give it your full concentration.

FRED. I've never been much for games. *(HE pulls out a new toaster.)* Look what I bought.

GILES. What was the matter with our old toaster?

FRED. It burnt one side of the bread black and left the other white as a miner's bum.

GILES. I liked it that way.

FRED. Of course we won't be able to use it until I get the plug on. *(Putting toaster on dresser.)* Can you tell me why, when you buy an electrical appliance, they can't have the plug already attached?

GILES. *(Vaguely; looking in bag.)* They've always done it that way. Did you get a paper?

FRED. In there. Two posh ones for you and a fun one for me.

GILES. (*Taking them out.*) Don't know how you can read that rubbish.

FRED. (*Takes newspapers, glances at headlines.*) Giles, be honest, which do you think is more interesting? (*Reads.*) "New Mortgage Rates Bring Relief To Economy" or . . . (*From other paper.*) "Randy Bishop Beds One-Legged Choirmistress"?

GILES. I suppose it depends on whether one's interest lies in real estate or religion. Anyway, I was really looking for the local. I thought there might be a photo.

FRED. (*Handing him paper.*) Here. I thought you hated having your picture taken.

GILES. It's not me I'm interested in, it's my vegetable marrows. Ah, here it is. (*Pleased.*) "Giles St. James takes a first with his marrows." Gave them almost three paragraphs. Picture doesn't really do them justice though.

FRED. (*Looking over his shoulder.*) But it's not bad of you. Mind you, the caption sounds a bit rude. (*Reading.*) "Giles Showing Off His Prize Marrows."

GILES. (*Moving away; still studying paper.*) They'd look better in color.

FRED. I got a nice piece of cod and some bath buns to have with our tea. And some wine to celebrate.

GILES. Celebrate what?

FRED. Look, I can't, for the life of me, see how anyone can get worked up over a pair of swollen marrows, but I know it means a lot to you.

GILES. (*Embarrassed.*) Yes, well—five seconds in a row. Nice to finally get the Blue Ribbon. Oh, it's not really the marrows, it's—well, the—recognition by one's—peers.

FRED. (*Affectionately.*) Did anyone ever tell you you're quite peculiar?

GILES. Hardly a day goes by.

FRED. I'll put the kettle on for tea. (*HE moves to switch radio on.*) Be a good chap and set the table. (*As we hear an old WALTZ.*) Oh, that one takes me back. (*HE picks up bags of groceries.*) Let me know if they say anything about the weather. (*FRED exits to kitchen.*)

(*GILES moves to table, picks up his marrows, looks at them admiringly; and then, happily clutching them to his chest, proceeds to waltz around the room.*

At this point, we see the slightly damp faces of LIBBY DANIELS and DAISY HOLIDAY appear at one of the windows. Quite nonplussed, THEY watch Giles dance with his marrows. When HE sees them, HE stops dead in his tracks, stares in surprise and acute embarrassment. LIBBY gives him a little finger wave. Still clutching the marrows, HE moves to open door to reveal the two women.)

GILES. Yes?

LIBBY. Hey, sorry to interrupt your—what you were doing—but we've got a bit of an emergency here.

GILES. What kind of emergency?

LIBBY. Our car went off the road and we ended up in a ditch about two hundred yards from here, with mud up the kazoo. My fault—it's a rental and I wasn't used to driving on the wrong side of the road. Anyway, I tried to gun it and maybe I flooded the engine, because it packed up on us.

GILES. You're American.
LIBBY. Is it okay if we come in anyway?
GILES. What? Oh yes—yes. I supposed you'd better.

(HE steps aside and THEY enter. LIBBY is a New Yorker
probably in her fifties to early sixties. Her insecurities
are usually effectively disguised, but when her defenses
slip, she can be very endearing.
DAISY HOLIDAY is a pretty woman in her twenties, with
an appealing, enthusiastic attitude towards life. SHE
speaks with a distinctive North Carolina accent which,
along with her wide-eyed optimism, sometimes causes
people to underestimate her intelligence.
GILES closes the door. There is an awkward pause. LIBBY
indicates the marrows HE is still holding.)

LIBBY. So how long have you and Ginger been
together?
GILES. What?
LIBBY. You and your friends dance very well.
GILES. (Embarrassed.) They're my prize marrows.
LIBBY. They're very—attractive.
GILES. (Awkwardly.) Yes, well, I was just putting
them away.
LIBBY. Look, I didn't mean to embarrass you. We all
do crazy things when we're alone.
GILES. (Not really a question.) Really?

(SHE shrugs. HE moves to turn off the radio but because
he is holding the marrows can't manage it.)

LIBBY. You want me to hold those for you?

(SHE moves to him. Somewhat reluctantly, HE hands them over to her. This produces a physical contact which further embarrasses him. HE avoids her eyes, turns off RADIO, faces her, takes marrows back from her.)

GILES. Thank you.

LIBBY. *(Straight-faced.)* It was a privilege.

GILES. *(Moves away to deposit marrows, turns back.)* Look, I'm not sure how we can be of any help.

LIBBY. Well, I thought maybe we could use your phone to call a tow truck.

GILES. The nearest garage is in Farnham, which is miles away.

LIBBY. He doesn't make house calls?

GILES. You're quite off the beaten track, you know.

DAISY. That was me. I'm a borderline fool when it comes to reading maps. You think two travellers in distress could prevail on your masculine expertise to get the engine started again?

GILES. *(Not succumbing to her charm.)* Yes, well, I don't have the faintest idea of how to repair a car; but perhaps Fred can take a look. I'll get him.

(As soon as HE leaves, their attitude changes.)

DAISY. Well, we're in!! You think it's him?

LIBBY. We don't even know if who we're looking for is a man.

(*During the following, the TWO quickly move around examining the room, perusing the books and even going so far as to open desk drawers.*)

DAISY. You think he suspects anything? I mean, he sure didn't rush to pour the bourbon and get the ribs on the barbecue.

LIBBY. Doesn't mean a thing. He's just English. They don't like people coming into their house.

DAISY. Why not?

LIBBY. Beats the hell out of me. Hospitality is just not part of their culture.

DAISY. (*Stops her search for a moment, looks around room.*) God, this place is so *cute*. It's everything I imagined an English cottage to be.

LIBBY. Yeah, well, don't get carried away—it's not typical. Those miles of grim, depressing, grey council flats and stucco semi-detacheds we passed on the way down here is the real England. God, it's freezing in here!

DAISY. Yeah, maybe it's my imagination, but it seemed warmer outside than in.

LIBBY. It's not your imagination. Ever since we landed at Heath Row, I've been freezing my buns off.

DAISY. Don't they have central heating?

LIBBY. Yeah, but they don't use it. They just save it for special occasions, like pneumonia.

DAISY. (*Stops her activities.*) Well, we may have struck out. Not a single book on murder in his whole library. There's nothing in this room that would make a hound dog twitch a whisker.

LIBBY. Well, we'll find out soon enough.

DAISY. How?

LIBBY. I'm going to ask him. (*SHE looks at her for a moment.*)

DAISY. Look, Libby, I know you're a "bottom line" sort of gal and all, but maybe in this situation it would be better if you, you know, got him to like you first.

LIBBY. (*Dryly.*) We don't have that much time.

DAISY. You know, you've got to stop putting yourself down like that.

LIBBY. Daisy, we don't have *time* for any games. We're down to our last credit card. If we don't pull this off today, we're out of business.

DAISY. But if he's kept his identity a secret all these years, why do you think he'll admit anything to us?

LIBBY. Money.

DAISY. (*Holding a framed photo, turns with a big grin.*) Bingo. (*As LIBBY looks at her.*) We may be in the right place. Theatrical photos.

(*FRED, wearing a sou'wester, enters.*)

FRED. Sorry to keep you waiting, my dears, but for some reason, the garage is not answering their phone. Giles is having another go. I'm Fred Craddock.

LIBBY. Hi, Fred. This is Daisy Holiday and I'm Libby Daniels.

FRED. Ah, lovely to hear American voices again.

LIBBY. Again?

FRED. I had some of the best times of my life in your country.

LIBBY. You think you can help us with the car?

FRED. Well, can't promise anything, love. I can just about get the bonnet open. After that, I know Sweet Fanny

Adams. (*Notices that DAISY is holding photo.*) Ah, I see you've uncovered some of my lurid past.

DAISY. I beg your pardon?

FRED. (*As HE moves to her.*) Hard to tell, but the callow, young sprout lurking in the background of all those photos is yours truly.

DAISY. You were an actor?

FRED. Well, aren't you sweet. No—well, I didn't have the face for it, did I?

(*GILES enters from kitchen.*)

FRED. No, I was more what you'd call behind the scenes—a dresser. Worked with Giles's dad for close to forty years. (*Pointing at photo.*) That's him there. (*He hands LIBBY the photo.*) And that's his mum—they appeared together a lot.

LIBBY. (*To Giles.*) Derek and Virginia St. James were your parents?

GILES. (*Surprised.*) You've heard of them?

LIBBY. Why are you so surprised? They were very famous.

GILES. But only in this country. They only played in New York once, and that was just after World War II.

LIBBY. Then I probably saw one of their movies.

GILES. They only made a few films and they weren't released outside of Britain.

LIBBY. Yes, well, I'm fairly knowledgeable about show business.

GILES. Oh, really?

LIBBY. It's my job. I used to—I produce movies.

FRED. (*Impressed.*) You do? In Hollywood?

LIBBY. A few.

FRED. Well, bless your heart.

LIBBY. Television mostly.

DAISY. She's one of the most talented and successful producers in the business. She's just not one to brag on herself.

GILES. That's very surprising.

(As THEY look at him.)

GILES. Modesty is not an American trait.

(A slight pause.)

LIBBY. You know, you could break an ankle jumping to those sort of conclusions.

GILES. I simply meant that your country invented hyperbole.

DAISY. This isn't hyperbole, sir. Writers *fight* to have her produce their scripts. She's helped a *lot* of people make a *lot* of money.

GILES. *(Unimpressed.)* Oh, really.

DAISY. If I'm lying I'm dying.

GILES. What?

DAISY. Southern expression.

GILES. Ah.

FRED. Well, we're going to have a high old time. I've always been dead keen on the films. Perhaps you can tell me—I've often wondered about Bette Davis. Was she—

GILES. Fred, perhaps you should look at the car before it gets dark.

FRED. Right, we can natter to our hearts' content later.

DAISY. I'll come with you. I have the keys.

(As THEY prepare to leave.)

FRED. When did you get here then?
DAISY. Just three days ago.
FRED. Oh dear, been nothing but drizzle. I wish you'd come in the summer. The rain's much warmer then.

(THEY exit. There is a slightly awkward pause.)

GILES. Yes—well, perhaps I should try and get through to the garage again.

*(During following, HE dials phone as LIBBY wanders to
    fireplace.)*

LIBBY. Is this a working fireplace?
GILES. Yes, but we only use it in the winter months, when it gets coolish.
LIBBY. Right.
GILES. Well, there's no point in simply chucking one's money around. Look, if you're feeling chilly, I *could* light it.
LIBBY. (*Hugging herself.*) No, it's okay. It's— character building.

*(HE glances sharply at her as HE picks up on her mild
    sarcasm.)*

GILES. Well, that's odd. Now nobody is answering. They've probably gone home. (*HE moves to fireplace, bends down to light fire through following.*) Is your enthusiastic young friend also a film producer?

LIBBY. You make it sound like a social disease.

GILES. Film producing?

LIBBY. Enthusiasm.

GILES. Do I?

LIBBY. She wants to learn the film business, so I exploit her shamelessly and call her my assistant.

GILES. Would I have seen any of the films you produced, Miss Daniels?

LIBBY. Call me Libby.

GILES. Ah, yes, I forgot about the American habit of instant familiarity.

LIBBY. Something wrong with that?

GILES. (*Shrugs.*) If one encourages every Tom, Dick and Harry to use one's Christian name, what are one's close friends supposed to call one? I don't think this is drawing properly.

LIBBY. Maybe the damper is closed.

GILES. No, that wouldn't be it.

LIBBY. (*Kneels down beside him.*) Here, let me check.

(*HE is conscious of her closeness.*)

LIBBY. Yeah, that's it.

GILES. Fred must have closed it.

LIBBY. (*Opens dampers, notices him staring at her.*) What is it?

GILES. What? Oh, it's your—aroma.

LIBBY. I beg your pardon?

GILES. Uh—perfume.

LIBBY. Too strong?

GILES. No. It's just that we're not used to pleasant smells in here.

LIBBY. I'm sorry to hear that.

GILES. (*Adds more wood to fire, turns to find her watching him.*) You didn't tell me if I might have been exposed to your films.

LIBBY. Do you go to the movies much?

GILES. Not really.

LIBBY. Then it's pretty unlikely.

GILES. I sometimes watch television. At least Fred does, so it's hard to escape it completely. (*HE lights cigarette.*) Oh, sorry, would you like one?

LIBBY. I don't smoke.

GILES. Of course not. You're not one of those people who wave their arms around when someone else does, are you?

LIBBY. (*Evenly.*) Not in other people's homes. What sort of things does he watch?

GILES. Who? Oh, Fred—oh, he has no will power at all—he'll watch anything.

LIBBY. Yeah, I guess TV is the same the world over.

GILES. Oh really?

LIBBY. Yeah, you know—"popcorn for the eyes."

GILES. That's not really true here. Most of our programmes have an educational thrust.

LIBBY. Yes, I actually managed to find a British made programme on last night. Told me more about pond life in Dorset than I thought possible.

GILES. Yes, well, we try not to confuse popularity with quality.

LIBBY. Sometimes it's possible to have both.

GILES. (*Turns away to stub his cigarette.*) Did that ever happen to you?

LIBBY. Only a couple of times. I once did a series based on Josephine Tey stories.

(*HE turns to look at her with some surprise.*)

LIBBY. What is it?

GILES. Those were quite good.

LIBBY. (*Surprised.*) You saw them?

GILES. I remember the series quite well. That was back—when?—in the mid-seventies, wasn't it?

LIBBY. Yes.

GILES. Have you done anything I might have seen since then?

LIBBY. Nothing worth throwing my hat in the air about.

GILES. Oh?

LIBBY. The networks never gave me that sort of material to work with again.

GILES. Why not?

LIBBY. (*Shrugs.*) Maybe I ruffled too many feathers.

GILES. (*Dryly.*) Hard to imagine.

LIBBY. Yeah, I know. I got a motor mouth.

GILES. Motor mouth?

LIBBY. I tend to speak before I think.

GILES. If it troubles you, why don't you stop?

LIBBY. Because then I wouldn't be me.

GILES. Would that be such a loss?

LIBBY. You know, you're not going to win any medals in the tact department either.

GILES. Really?

LIBBY. Really.

GILES. Yes, I suppose I have been accused of dropping a few bricks from time to time.

LIBBY. Better than most Englishmen who don't give anything away.

GILES. Oh?

LIBBY. You ask a simple question like "Where are you from?" and they get real nervous.

GILES. That's not such a simple question.

LIBBY. "Where are you from?"

GILES. An answer could give away a great deal of personal information—one's background, financial status, schooling—

LIBBY. Yeah, that would really let the cat out of the bag, wouldn't it?

GILES. Our reticence bothers you?

LIBBY. You mean secrecy.

GILES. What makes you believe we're secretive?

LIBBY. Well, for one thing, you don't even put your return address on the outside of your mail.

GILES. So?

LIBBY. How can your letters be returned if they go astray?

GILES. They don't. We trust our postal system. Also we tend to value our privacy more than most.

LIBBY. Even in death.

GILES. Death?

LIBBY. In the newspaper obits they never print how a person died.

GILES. That information is important to you?

LIBBY. Especially at my age.

GILES. But *why*?

LIBBY. I want to know what to look out for. Aren't you curious about why a person checked out?

GILES. Not enough to invade their privacy.

LIBBY. They're dead. How they going to know?

GILES. It's still their business if they want to keep anything personal to themselves.

LIBBY. Yeah, that's probably why the British make such good spies. You're comfortable with masks.

GILES. You think so? The fire's coming along nicely. (*HE moves to warm his hands.*) What brings you to this part of the country?

LIBBY. I'm trying to track down a literary hero—or heroine, I'm not sure—of mine.

GILES. Who would that be?

LIBBY. T.J. Walbourne.

GILES. (*Turns to look at her.*) The mystery writer?

LIBBY. Oh, I think he's much more than that, don't you?

GILES. In what way?

LIBBY. He writes full-blooded, three-dimensional characters—specific, idiosyncratic, original. He also has great humour—another rare quality—and, of course, intelligence. But perhaps most important—compassion. (*A beat.*) You don't agree?

GILES. I couldn't say. I've never read any of his books.

LIBBY. I've read all twenty-three of them. About five times each.

GILES. Is this a recent obsession?

LIBBY. No, I fell in love with him a long time ago. At first I was just turned on by the sex, you know.

GILES. Ah.

LIBBY. Yeah, I figure this guy either has a private life that would make Warren Beatty blush, or he's unbelievably repressed with a depraved, fevered imagination.

GILES. Oh, really?

LIBBY. Look. All I know is that when I read him, I had to keep taking showers. (*GILES blushes slightly.*) Anyway, the affair still burns brightly.

(THEY are looking at one another as FRED and DAISY, a bit mud-spattered and damp, enter. THEY are carrying suitcases from the car.)

FRED. Well, that was a proper cock up. Excuse my French, my dear.

GILES. No luck?

FRED. No joy at all. Motor's dead as Marley's ghost. It's coming down in buckets, so the mud is up over the axle. We're going to need a tow to pull her out. Did you call the garage again?

GILES. They're not answering.

FRED. Well, that's a bit of a rum go. Still—not to worry. If worse comes to worse, I can run you into town myself. (*To Daisy.*) Here, let me get that coat off you, love. (*As HE helps her out of coat.*) Oh, I see you've got a nice fire going. You sit over there and warm up while I get tea started. You two must be famished.

DAISY. We don't want to put you to any trouble.

FRED. Don't be daft. We can do with a spot of company. Besides, it'll give me a chance to pay back some old debts.

LIBBY. Debts?

FRED. Yes. You see, many years ago, in 1946—no, I tell a lie—it was forty-seven, when I was in New York—

GILES. I'll get those suitcases out of the way.

FRED. That'd be a big help, old chap.

(As GILES exits with suitcases:)

FRED. For some reason, Giles doesn't like me talking about my time over there. Now if you ladies would like to freshen up, the w.c. is just up the stairs and to the left.

DAISY. Thanks. I would like to get some of the mud off.

FRED. Just don't expect too much in the way of creature comforts. Over here we keep the heat off in the loo and the windows wide open, so it seems as much like an army latrine as possible.

DAISY. *(Puzzled.)* Why?

FRED. To remind us of the war.

DAISY. That's a fond memory?

FRED. Oh yes, we all miss it terribly. *(HE exits.)*

DAISY. Well, he's just adorable, but I don't think he's our guy. What about Giles? You learn anything?

LIBBY. It's tough. You can never tell what they mean by what they say. It's like cracking a code.

DAISY. How do they understand each other?

LIBBY. There are probably subtle clues they start learning in the cradle.

DAISY. You mean they have the key and we don't?

LIBBY. You got it. Sort of like the *London Times* crossword puzzle. *(SHE begins to check out the room.)*

DAISY. I thought we spoke the same language.

LIBBY. No way. They find it impossible to be direct. Listen to Giles—how he uses the impersonal "one" to distance himself. When they disagree, they don't say "You're full of shit!" They say "Oh, really?" or "Do you think so?"

DAISY. Gee, and I thought they were just being polite.

LIBBY. Honey, politeness has nothing to do with their consideration of other people. It's the embarrassment of just being.

DAISY. Being what?

LIBBY. English. Drives me nuts.

DAISY. But you think Giles could be our guy?

LIBBY. (*Shrugs.*) His mask is firmly clamped in place, so he could be. Well, there's nothing here. Come on, let's go upstairs and check out his medicine chest.

DAISY. England brings out the worst in you.

LIBBY. (*Grins.*) That's got nothing to do with England. I do that in everyone's bathroom.

(*THEY exit up the stairs.*
GILES enters, picks up Libby's coat, holds it for a second, becomes aware of her perfume, smells it, frowns, puzzled by his reaction, hangs it up . . . picks up wine bottle, opens it, pours a glass, sits by the fire and is sipping wine as FRED, carrying some food, enters.)

FRED. Looks as if you're ready to go to work again.

GILES. What makes you say that?

FRED. You're wearing your odd socks.

GILES. Not helping much.

FRED. Wine all right?

GILES. Haven't had a good hock in a long time.

FRED. You should get out more.

(GILES looks at him.)

FRED. Might help with that blockage of yours.

GILES. What? Oh, you mean "block." What has sex to do with that?

FRED. Your dad had a theory. He thought—now let me get this right—that a man's ability to create is tied in with his capacity to fall in love.

GILES. I don't see the connection.

FRED. Well, he said falling in love was what you might call a creative act. You had to imagine the loved one—so to speak—had all sorts of qualities they don't actually have. So when the ability to do that goes up the spout, all the other creative powers go on the fritz too.

GILES. *(Finally.)* Actors should not be allowed to say anything that isn't written down for them.

FRED. Oh, it was. It was from "An Act of the Imagination," a nice little play we toured in 1951. He practiced what he preached, too. That's why he kept working until well into his eighties. He was quite a lad with the ladies, was your dad—said that's what kept him going.

GILES. You mean he died when he could no longer take "yes" for an answer?

FRED. *(Grins and gives a little shrug.)* I think he might have had something there though. Anyway, worth a try, don't you think, old chap?

GILES. What's all this in aid of, Fred?

FRED. Oh, I don't know. Sometimes I think you're too good for your own good.

(As GILES looks at him.)

FRED. Look, I know you don't like to talk about this but don't you think you've been licking your wounds long enough?

GILES. Fred, my teeth are starting to wobble in their gums—

(FRED looks at him.)

GILES. I have what feels like a lobster residing in my lower back—I have a prostate I suspect is bigger than the diamond at the Ritz, I'm beginning to dribble—and you want me to *date?*

FRED. I haven't noticed you dribbling.

(GILES just looks at him as DAISY and LIBBY come down the stairs.)

FRED. Almost ready, ladies. Let me pour you a glass of wine. *(As HE does.)* So are you two on holiday then?

GILES. Miss Daniels and Miss Holiday are searching for an author—what's his name again?

LIBBY. T.J. Walbourne.

FRED. Well, fancy that. So what do you want with him then?

LIBBY. I want to get the TV rights to his novels.

GILES. I don't recall seeing any of his work on television, do you, Fred?

FRED. No—lots of P.D. James and Ruth Rendel, but no T.J. Walbourne—no, wait a minute, I tell a lie. There was one, donkey's years ago. Proper cock up it was.

GILES. If he hasn't given permission before, what makes you think he'll let you acquire the rights?

LIBBY. Well, I was hoping my charm might do it.

GILES. Seriously.

(THEY look at him.)

GILES. What?

FRED. Don't mind him. He's not really rude. He just doesn't get out much, so he's lost the knack of what you might call social intercourse. Now everybody grab a plate and help yourself.

DAISY. Why do you think he hasn't let anyone film his work?

(THEY all help themselves to food, find places to sit throughout the following.)

GILES. Who? Oh, T.J. Walbourne? I have no idea. But I'm sure he has his reasons.

DAISY. Like what?

GILES. Privacy.

LIBBY. I have something to offer that's better than privacy.

GILES. What might that be?

LIBBY. Fame.

GILES. A dubious achievement.

LIBBY. Okay—money.

GILES. I would assume he's been offered money before.

LIBBY. Not the sort of money he could make with me. The series would start on American prime time television—I already have that commitment if I get the rights—and that would mean world-wide syndication. We're talking millions of dollars here.

GILES. What makes you think this person even lives in this part of the country?

DAISY. (*Excited.*) We just put together a lot of clues—from his books—the subjects he wrote about, for instance—and then proceeded on the basis that he'd be a person interested in those subjects. Like, well, cricket, which he used in "Death At The Oval" or the four books using the background of show business—you know, "This'll Kill You" or "Murder Above The Title"—or gardening, which is featured in most of his books. Okay, so we now had a profile of what sort of person he may be. I then had a hunch that his pen name might be an anagram for the town or village he—

GILES. That's all complete rubbish.

DAISY. Excuse me?

GILES. If this person is so determined not to be located one would assume he has brains enough not to provide clues that would lead to his privacy being shattered. And, even if, by some chance, you did run him to earth what makes you believe that he would trust his work to two total strangers?

DAISY. Because we both *idolize* his talent, and Libby would protect his work to the death and it would be transferred to TV in an artistic, *tasteful* manner.

GILES. Yes—well, your faith in your employees is admirable but—why are you telling me all this?

DAISY. I guess we were hoping that you may know where Mr. Walbourne is and put in a good word for us.

GILES. Miss Holiday—

DAISY. Daisy.

GILES. Yes ... even if I did know this T.L. Walbourne—

DAISY. J.

GILES. What?

DAISY. T.J.

GILES. Ah. Well, I wouldn't presume to intrude upon his privacy. I'm sorry, that sort of thing just isn't done.

(We hear a CLAP OF THUNDER and HEAVY RAIN.)

GILES. Do you have any reservations for the night?

(DAISY shakes her head.)

GILES. Well, there's only one hotel in this area. Fred, perhaps you should call the inn and see if they have a room available. You want me to look up the number?

FRED. No, I know the number. I'll put the kettle on for tea.

DAISY. I'll give you a hand.

(THEY exit.)

GILES. Fred can run you down to the inn.

LIBBY. (*Has been studying Giles.*) You're wearing odd socks.

GILES. I know.

LIBBY. Fashion statement?

GILES. It started as a mistake, became a superstition and then—

LIBBY. An affectation?

GILES. A habit.

LIBBY. Ah. My God, now you've got me doing it.

(HE doesn't understand.)

LIBBY. Superstition about what?

GILES. My work I suppose.

LIBBY. What is your work?

GILES. I'm semi-retired.

LIBBY. From what?

GILES. This and that.

LIBBY. Do you always wear the red on the right foot and the green on the left?

(FRED enters, moves to get tea caddy.)

GILES. Look, it's hardly worth discussing.

LIBBY. Why not? I love eccentricities. That's one thing I like about English villages. They tolerate eccentrics.

GILES. We don't have any eccentrics in our village.

FRED. Oh, what about old Tom then?

GILES. Tom?

FRED. Tom Partridge—down at the pub.

LIBBY. In what way is he eccentric?

FRED. He thinks he's a poached egg.

(HE exits to kitchen.
LIBBY looks at Giles.)

GILES. Fred is given to exaggeration.

LIBBY. Tom doesn't think he's a poached egg?

GILES. Not all the time.

(SHE waits but he is not forthcoming.)

LIBBY. Uh—how do people know when he thinks he's a poached egg?

GILES. Well, if you must know, he carries this small brown mat around with him. That's his toast. He sits in the middle of it and nobody is allowed to tread on his toast.

LIBBY. Amazing.

GILES. Look, it's not that strange. Nobody makes a fuss about it. Everyone needs something to keep people away.

LIBBY. *(Looks at him for a moment.)* What's *your* story, Giles? You're an axe murderer who doesn't want to be discovered? You ran out on your family and don't want them to find you? I mean, what are the reasons for living like a Tibetan monk?

GILES. They're personal.

LIBBY. I'm getting on a plane tomorrow. Who am I going to tell? I mean, what's the big deal?

GILES. *(A slight shrug.)* We tend to be somewhat more reserved than you Americans.

LIBBY. *(Out of patience.)* Oh yeah, the famous English reserve. Well, that could be described in another way.

GILES. How?

LIBBY. Death in life.

GILES. *(Stung.)* Because we don't flaunt our emotions? Because we don't practically stop strangers on the street and confess our innermost thoughts like your countrymen?

LIBBY. Tell me something? Is it just me who grates on you or do you dislike all Americans?

GILES. I could say that you don't seem overly fond of the British.

LIBBY. But you wouldn't. That would be much too personal. Anyway, I asked you first.

GILES. (*Tightly controlled.*) Yes, well, for my tastes, I find Americans a trifle too—intense.

(SHE casually puts her hands on his shoulders.)

LIBBY. (*Dryly.*) That's right, bubbula—let it all out.

(HE quickly moves away from this contact and his facade finally cracks. HE doesn't totally lose control, but is on his way.)

GILES. All right! I loathe your worship of the almighty dollar! I hate what you've done to the English language! I am deeply offended by your excesses, your waste and your careless pollution of the atmosphere! I detest your obsession with what is new at the expense of tradition! I believe that your infantile concept that bigger is better is disgusting! I find that your belief that the acme of culture is Disneyland ridiculous. I abhor your foreign policy of invading any country just because you don't like their government! I believe your killing of hundreds and thousands of people in needless wars and then holding victory parades despicable! I deplore your exploitation of mindless violence in films and find your sentimentality only slightly less offensive. I detest rock n' roll, McDonald's, T-shirts with asinine messages, freeways, baseball caps, standing ovations, stealth bombers, and Mickey Mouse! But most of all, I am disgusted by the attitude that wealth and power can buy anything or anybody! In short: I hate everything the United States represents!

(SHE is so shocked by this outburst, SHE is rendered uncharacteristically speechless for a moment.
As THEY are staring at one another, FRED enters.)

FRED. Good news!

(THEY turn to look at him.)

FRED. They don't have any rooms available, so the two ladies will be brightening our lives tonight. (*To the still speechless Libby.*) We don't have many visitors, so it'll be a proper treat—won't it, Giles?

CURTAIN

End of ACT I, Scene 1

ACT I

Scene 2

About noon the next day.

LIBBY, wearing a sweat suit, enters through the front door. SHE is panting slightly and it is obvious that she has

*been running. SHE takes the jacket off and we see that
the T-shirt underneath bears the legend "Whoever has
the most things when they die wins." SHE then
proceeds to launch into some stretching exercises.*

*GILES enters from upstairs, stops and, unnoticed by her,
stands observing Libby's not unattractive rear end move
up and down. SHE notices him watching her, stops,
looks at him.*

GILES. (*Tries to cover his embarrassment.*) You know,
none of us are going to get out of this thing alive.
LIBBY. What?
GILES. Life. You Americans think that if you run ten
miles a day, don't eat meat, don't drink or smoke, you'll
live forever. You seem to treat death as optional. Or a
personal failure.

*(SHE resumes stretching as HE moves to sit and lights a
cigarette.)*

LIBBY. Is there anything wrong with wanting to look
your best?
GILES. Americans don't want to look their best. They
want to look like film stars. That's why plastic surgeons
are your new heroes.
LIBBY. Everybody likes to look younger.
GILES. A face-lift doesn't make anyone look younger.
It just makes them look surprised. Anyway, I just think
that God may have got it right the first time.
LIBBY. You wouldn't say that if you'd seen me before I
had my face done.

(This takes him back for a second.)

GILES. I might have known.

LIBBY. *(Straightens up, notices him looking at her.)* What is it? You trying to find the scars?

GILES. No, I was just looking at your breasts— *(Quickly.)* I mean your chest—the writing on your chest. *(Reading.)* "Whoever has the most things when they die— wins." Is that a personal credo?

LIBBY. No, just someone's idea of a happy ending.

GILES. Oh yes, happy endings are very important to you, aren't they?

LIBBY. Yeah, we're pretty comfortable with happiness.

GILES. Pity it's unattainable.

LIBBY. We think it is. *(SHE resumes exercising.)*

GILES. Perhaps that's because you don't know how the world really works.

LIBBY. *(Stops exercising, looks at him.)* Why do you all dislike us?

GILES. Why would you think that?

LIBBY. Just a wild guess.

GILES. You're oversimplifying.

LIBBY. You're right. It's not simple dislike. It's a mixture of envy, disdain, grudging admiration and dismissal.

GILES. You may have a point, but did it ever occur to you that perhaps, just perhaps, we might have valid reasons for our attitudes?

LIBBY. *(Shrugs.)* The United States is very easy to poke fun at. We're a huge country with huge problems, but at least we're willing to make some changes.

GILES. All right, perhaps we're slower to change than you are. We've never had a revolution and—

LIBBY. Forget revolution. You never even had an *evolution*.

GILES. Yes, perhaps we are a trifle enamored with yesterday.

LIBBY. The day before yesterday. When I come here, I always set my watch back three hundred years.

GILES. I think you're conveniently ignoring what Britain has given the world, Miss Daniels.

LIBBY. Libby, for Christ's sake. Libby! What did you have in mind?

GILES. Our legal system, our medical discoveries, literature including the greatest writer the world has ever known, brilliant theatre, great painters and wonderful architecture.

LIBBY. Not to mention Andrew Lloyd Webber.

GILES. I think I need a drink. (*HE moves to pour himself a glass.*) Would you like one? Oh, I forgot—you don't drink either.

LIBBY. Noticed that, did you?

GILES. Hard not to when you make such a show of turning your glass upside down. Is that also part of your attempt to stay ever slim, ever young?

LIBBY. No, I'm a recovering alcoholic.

GILES. (*Thrown, HE looks at her.*) What?

LIBBY. I was a lush.

(*As HE stares at her.*)

LIBBY. I had a sizeable problem with booze.

GILES. I'm—I'm terribly sorry.

LIBBY. Yeah, well, there's a lot of people from my past who feel the same way.

GILES. No, I meant I'm sorry that I—

LIBBY. I know. I was attempting a little humour. You know—irony. I thought you guys were big on irony.

GILES. We are. We just don't expect it from an American.

(SHE grins. Awkwardly.)

GILES. Well, it's nice that you can laugh about it.

LIBBY. Smile. I'm working up to laugh. No questions?

GILES. About what?

LIBBY. My drinking.

GILES. Good Lord, no.

LIBBY. Too personal, huh?

GILES. Well, I understand your feeling that.

LIBBY. I meant for you.

GILES. Uh, no—well, yes—I mean—*(Holds up glass.)* Look, does this bother you?

LIBBY. Of course not. Just because the string on my own guitar broke doesn't mean the tune has stopped for everyone. Anyway, I've been sober for three years now.

GILES. Ah.

LIBBY. And you're wondering why I'm telling you all this. *(As HE gives an awkward shrug.)* That's okay—so am I. Oh shit, maybe it's because I thought before I leave, it might be nice to relate as two human beings.

GILES. What made you stop drinking?

LIBBY. Well, what do you know—finally, a question.

GILES. You don't have to answer.

LIBBY. I hit bottom. I got into a horrendous car accident.

GILES. Were you hurt?

LIBBY. My face was really banged up. Just to make you feel bad—*that's* when I had the plastic surgery.

GILES. *Now* I'm embarrassed.

LIBBY. Anyway, that's when Dan—that's my husband—divorced me.

GILES. You have children?

LIBBY. Yes—a daughter. You?

GILES. No, I chose—not to.

LIBBY. Oh?

GILES. I didn't have a particularly—joyful childhood.

LIBBY. Who did?

GILES. You neither?

LIBBY. Awkward.

GILES. Awkward?

LIBBY. When I was twelve years old I was the height I am now.

GILES. Ah. That made you shy?

LIBBY. No. Pushy.

GILES. What age is your daughter?

LIBBY. She's a college senior.

GILES. She lives with you in New York?

LIBBY. No, with her father. (*Too casually.*) When we split Dan got custody.

GILES. That must have been—difficult.

LIBBY. It was. Still is.

GILES. Still?

LIBBY. We have some problems to work out.

GILES. Problems?

LIBBY. She won't talk to me.

GILES. Ah. Well, I'm sure you will eventually.
LIBBY. I'll drink to that.
GILES. What? Oh, yes—I see. (*HE moves away to attend to the fire.*)

(*SHE throws herself into some vigorous exercises.*)

GILES. (*Looking up chimney.*) I don't think this chimney has been swept since World War Two.
LIBBY. Fred thinks the British still miss the war.
GILES. Fred spent too long with my parents. He became infected with an overdose of theatricality.
LIBBY. Were you in the war, Giles?
GILES. Well, I was a trifle too young to be "in" the war, as in the armed services. (*Still tending fire.*) As a child, I experienced some of the London blitz though.
LIBBY. One of my favorite books took place during the London blitz. I read it years ago—*Murder in the Blackout*—that was the title. Absolutely brilliant. Man wanted to kill his wife, so he crept into the house and shot her during an air raid. Of course nobody heard the sound of the shot because—
GILES. (*Irritated.*) No, no, no—that wasn't the plot at all. He was a soldier—a bomb expert—and he planted a *bomb* in the house programmed to go off during the air raid and blow up the entire house. That was what was so brilliant. It looked as if a *German* bomb had struck the house, and so nobody suspected it was a murder.

(*A pause, which causes HIM to turn and look at LIBBY who has stopped exercising and is gazing at him.*)

LIBBY. (*Finally.*) I thought you said you'd never read any T.J. Walbourne.

(*Another pause, and then surprisingly, GILES, both feet together, starts bouncing all over the room in a mixture of self-hate and total frustration.*)

GILES. Damn, damn, damn, damn, damn, damn, damn, damn, damn!!!!! (*HE finally stops.*)

(*LIBBY has been watching this astonishing display with a somewhat smug smile.*)

LIBBY. It's okay, Giles. I always knew you were T.J. Walbourne.

GILES. Rubbish—you tricked me! How—how could you possibly know that's who I was?

LIBBY. I bribed someone.

GILES. (*Shocked.*) What?

LIBBY. That's my style.

GILES. Style?

LIBBY. I like to "cut to the chase."

GILES. Who was it? Someone working at my publishers—someone in my agent's office?

LIBBY. Does that matter?

GILES. Yes, to me it's important.

LIBBY. Why?

GILES. It involves a breach of trust.

LIBBY. I can't tell you.

GILES. Why not?

LIBBY. It would be a breach of trust. I'm sorry.

GILES. So am I. I'd counted on their loyalty.

LIBBY. Money talks.

GILES. Perhaps not as loudly as you believe. I'm not interested in your proposal.

LIBBY. We're talking about an awful lot of money here.

GILES. I have enough money.

LIBBY. Nobody has enough money. And this would make you famous.

GILES. As what? A hack writer of some tatty television series?

LIBBY. It wouldn't be tacky.

GILES. I've seen how books are mutilated by American TV.

LIBBY. That wouldn't be true in this case because you'd be writing the scripts yourself.

GILES. I don't know a thing about screenwriting.

LIBBY. No, but I do. We'd be collaborators.

GILES. I can't imagine a worse nightmare.

LIBBY. What? Working with me? Going to the States and becoming a billionaire? Having millions of people see your work and maybe going out and buying your books? Which part of that is a nightmare?

GILES. All of it.

LIBBY. Does that mean you want to think about it?

GILES. No. It's quite out of the question.

LIBBY. Okay. How about immortality?

GILES. God, you'll promise anything, won't you?

LIBBY. No, that's my final offer. It could all happen, you know.

GILES. You expect too much from life.

LIBBY. And you expect too little.

(HE breaks their contact and starts to move away.

    LIBBY. (*Suddenly yells.*) Don't move.

(Completely nonplussed, HE freezes.)

    LIBBY. Stay where you are! Don't take a step! (*Peering at floor.*) I've lost one of my contact lenses.
    GILES. Oh, is that all? You know, a simple "sit and heel" would have been sufficient.
    LIBBY. Sorry, I tend to be a bit dramatic.
    GILES. I've never understood why people wear contact lenses.
    LIBBY. To look better. And don't give me that "God got it right the first time" because if He had, we wouldn't need contact lenses. (*SHE has found it.*) Ah, here it is. (*SHE licks it, is about to put it in her pocket.*)
    GILES. You're not going to put it back in?
    LIBBY. Not in front of you. It looks gross.
    GILES. Would you like me to avert my eyes?

(HE turns away; SHE sits cross-legged, proceeds to replace lens.)

    GILES. Funny, I wouldn't have thought you were the modest type.
    LIBBY. I'm as insecure as the next woman who's been dumped by her husband.
    GILES. Do you still see your ex-husband?
    LIBBY. Nope. It's weird.
    GILES. Oh?

LIBBY. Well, all the time I was married to Dan, I was drinking to various degrees. Like he never saw me totally sober, you know. Well, I've been sober for three years and he's never even bothered to see me. Wouldn't you think he'd be a little bit curious to see what I was really like when I was straight?

GILES. Yes.

(THEY make contact for a moment.)

LIBBY. Listen, will you answer just one question?

(HE doesn't answer.)

LIBBY. I was lying in bed last night thinking of all the reasons you'd have for not giving me the rights to your work, and the most important seems to be the protection of your privacy. Am I right?

GILES. Yes.
LIBBY. Why?

(A slight pause.)

GILES. Is it really so important to you?
LIBBY. You bet.
GILES. And if I tell you—no more questions?
LIBBY. You got it.
GILES. *(Considers for a moment, sits opposite her on the floor.)* I hate celebrity.
LIBBY. Why?
GILES. Because I've seen what it does to people.

(SHE waits. HE decides to go on.)

GILES. All right. As you know, my parents were a famous acting team and when I was a child, our house was always filled with other public figures—larger than life creatures whose lives were chronicled by media and who seemed to live only for the next time their photographs would be in the papers or when they would give their next television interview. Even as a small boy, it struck me as an—unsatisfactory way to spend one's life.

LIBBY. But how did it affect you?

GILES. In every way. I was sent away to boarding school, but because of my parents' notoriety, I was marked as being—different. Oh, there were other sons of famous men in school, but they were—respectably famous— diplomats, financial tycoons, that sort of thing, and they weren't constantly in the daily tabloids or making jokes on TV chat shows. Also, they didn't have the "glittering charm" of my father, so their children weren't expected to live up to an image of witty sophistication. As you may have noticed, I am not a charming man—and I was not a charming child. (*As SHE goes to speak.*) It's all right, you don't have to be polite.

LIBBY. Politeness is not one of my virtues, Giles. But maybe you're being hard on yourself.

GILES. No, simply accurate. (*As SHE goes to speak.*) Please, I know myself better than you. Where was I?

LIBBY. Your folks. Didn't you spend any time at home?

GILES. Just the holidays, but since my parents were usually working, I spent almost all my time in backstage dressing rooms, so I was rarely alone with either he or my mother. I never got to know who they really were because *they* had lost any real sense of who they were. I suppose that's what I hated most about what public exposure can do to one.

LIBBY. So when you started to be published, you decided to isolate yourself?

GILES. I'm not isolated. To the contrary, I'm part of the community here. Look, I'm a very odd duck; but slowly, over the years, I've managed to become accepted. I play on the village cricket team, I take part in the garden shows, and I have the odd pint at the local where everyone calls me Giles. Small pleasures, but I value them highly.

LIBBY. You think that would all change if they knew you were a famous writer?

GILES. Yes—because instead of being like them—just an ordinary chap muddling along making the best of things, I'd be regarded as some sort of—exotic creature, and they'd start treating me differently. That would spoil everything. You see, I've never really belonged anywhere before. (*A beat.*) Do you understand any of this?

LIBBY. Of course.

GILES. Really?

LIBBY. We all want to belong somewhere.

GILES. Then you can understand why I can't give you the rights to my work?

LIBBY. Yes. Don't think I'm not pissed off about it, but I understand. I just wish you'd revealed your big secret before.

GILES. What big secret?

LIBBY. That, you're human.

GILES. (*Embarrassed, HE lapses back into formality.*) Yes, well, I'm glad we had a chance to have this little chat.

(SHE nods, starts to get up, suddenly groans, grimaces and doubles over.)

    LIBBY. Oh, shit!
    GILES. *(Alarmed.)* What? What is it?
    LIBBY. A cramp—charley horse—my leg—please—grab my leg!
    GILES. I beg your—
    LIBBY. For God's sake—just do it!

(HE gingerly takes the calf of her leg in his hands.)

    LIBBY. No—harder—rub it harder— *(As HE does.)* Yeah, that's it—a bit higher.
    GILES. Feeling better?
    LIBBY. I didn't finish my stretch exercises and—yeah, that's good, that feels great—yeah.

(HE stops massaging her, but still keeps his hands on her leg.)

    GILES. I'm glad. I know a cramp can be very—

(HE suddenly grabs her and kisses her. THEY break. SHE is covered with confusion. HE does not show any visible reaction but, surprisingly, carries on talking as if nothing untoward has taken place.)

    GILES. —uh, painful. Of course, I was never one for strenuous sports. I went to—

(SHE watches, absolutely dumbfounded as HE moves away.)

GILES. —a number of different schools, mostly to avoid being ambushed by reporters who wanted to know about the state of my parents' marriage, but I was somewhat uncoordinated so I never became involved with—

(LIBBY raises her hand, but HE chooses not to see it.)

GILES. —sports. I'm afraid this made me rather the odd man out in school but—

LIBBY. Uh—excuse me.

GILES. Yes?

LIBBY. Am I crazy or did some physical contact take place a few moments ago?

GILES. Really?

LIBBY. I'm almost positive. Are you trying to say it escaped your attention?

GILES. Of course not. I—I just thought it was bad form to bring it up.

LIBBY. Bad form?

GILES. Look, do we have to talk about it? I mean, can't we just pretend it— *(HE suddenly kisses her again.)* I'm—I'm terribly sorry. I don't know why it—I really am *terribly* sorry.

LIBBY. *(Totally thrown.)* Hey, it's okay. I mean—it's okay.

(HE kisses her again.)

LIBBY. (*Flustered.*) Does this mean I get the rights?

(*HE looks at her unbelievingly.*)

LIBBY. Only kidding! Didn't mean it! Really—I'm a bit confused—I just can't put it all in—in my head yet.

GILES. I—know. I don't understand any of this either. I mean I was—was never one to let just my—er—physical urges—to rule my— (*HE kisses her urgently.*) My God, I can't believe this! I'm—*old*!!

LIBBY. (*Breathlessly.*) Well, it's nice that we finally found something we have in common.

GILES. The point is, I don't have a clue about how to act in a circumstance like this. I mean it's not even supposed to come up when one is this old. The situation, I mean. Do *you* have any idea what to do about—it?

LIBBY. Well, it's been a long time since I've actually *done* anything about it.

GILES. It has?

LIBBY. If I said that my love life over the past few years has been meagre, I'd be bragging.

GILES. I find that hard to believe.

LIBBY. Listen, I've almost forgotten where everything goes.

GILES. What?

LIBBY. Uh—the noses—that sort of thing.

GILES. Oh—yes, I know what you mean. Look, would you mind terribly if— (*HE kisses her.*)

LIBBY. Yes, that seems right. My God, I don't believe this is *happening*!

GILES. What next?

LIBBY. Listen, I'm out of practice at this sort of thing—there's blood pounding in my head and—look, even in my prime I was never exactly Madonna.

GILES. Who?

LIBBY. I never slept with anyone I hadn't had Thanksgiving dinner with. Look, would you do me a favor? Would you tell me to shut up before I ruin everything?

GILES. No, I need some help.

LIBBY. Well, if memory serves me—uh, we get a seedy room. Did I say the wrong thing again?

GILES. No, no—and we have one of those, but—well, we'll have to wait until Fred and Daisy are asleep—would that be all right?

LIBBY. Absolutely.

GILES. (*Kisses her, more gently this time.*) Yes—well—I suppose we should rest up.

LIBBY. Rest up? You think we need to go into *training*?

GILES. No, I just mean, if we're going to have to stay up until—well, maybe take a nap.

LIBBY. Oh, I'm too excited to sleep. (*SHE gets up, moves away.*) It reminds me of when I was a kid, before the July the Fourth picnic. I could never sleep then either.

GILES. You like picnics?

LIBBY. Fireworks.

GILES. Ah. Yes—see what you mean.

LIBBY. Have I embarrassed you again?

GILES. No—it's just that—well, talking about something could lead to one being disappointed.

LIBBY. How?

GILES. Well, one could be expecting rockets and only get a damp squib.

LIBBY. That's okay, I'll settle for a damp squib. Listen, I'll settle for a damp anything.

(HE starts to laugh; SHE joins him and their laughter builds until THEY fall into each other's arms.
FRED enters unnoticed, observes them.)

FRED. (*Pleased.*) I take it there'll be four for dinner then?

CURTAIN

End of ACT I, Scene 2

ACT 1

Scene 3

SCENE: Very early the next morning. Before the curtain goes up, we hear the SOUND OF SOMEONE POUNDING ON A TYPEWRITER.

AT RISE: We see it is GILES who has set up an old manual typewriter on the table and is typing, a contented smile on his face. A splash of color has been created by a low bowl of runiculas or asters on the table. FRED, his arms full of groceries, enters through front door, stands watching him.

FRED. Well, we're up early, aren't we?

GILES. (*Looks up.*) What? Oh, yes. Had a bit of a breakthrough.

FRED. I noticed.

GILES. I meant on the book.

FRED. Maybe your old dad was right.

GILES. Don't talk rubbish, Fred.

FRED. Who are the runiculas for then?

GILES. Nobody. Thought we could use a spot of color, that's all. What are you doing up and about so early?

FRED. I nipped into the village to get some supplies. Thought I'd have a go at cooking a real English meal for the ladies.

GILES. What's that?

FRED. Shepherd's pie and a nice pudding like Spotted Dick.

GILES. God help them.

FRED. It tastes better than it sounds, you know. Oh, I picked up the local paper.

GILES. Just put it over there.

(*As FRED moves to deposit it.*)

GILES. Did they ever repair the car?

FRED. Yes. There was a part missing. Turned out Libby had it in the pocket of her mackintosh.

GILES. She's very devious. They take the car back?

FRED. (*Nods.*) Well, they didn't need it anymore, did they? Now I'll get out of your way before you get stopped up again. (*HE heads for kitchen door, remembers something.*) Oh, by the way, were you smoking in bed last night?

GILES. Me?

FRED. Yes, I woke up about three and I swore I could smell cigarette smoke.

GILES. Well, maybe I did have a cigarette. I can't remember.

FRED. (*Nods, heads for door again.*) Oh, I almost forgot. (*Lowers his voice.*) I stopped off at the chemists.

GILES. Why are you whispering?

(*FRED puts a number of small condom packages on the table. Puzzled, GILES examines them.*)

GILES. What are these?

FRED. Condoms. While you were rusticating, they've come back in style.

GILES. Ah.

FRED. Well, you never know, do you?

GILES. Oh yes—yes, of course. Thank you, Fred.

FRED. Must say old Henry gave me a funny look. He probably thought I was indulging in some wishful thinking. Or maybe it was because I bought a packet in every size. (*As GILES looks at him.*) Well, I don't know you that well, do I?

GILES. (*Examining packets.*) Good Lord, they must have cost a fortune.

FRED. Can never spend too much on romance.

GILES. Well, perhaps we can exchange the ones that— aren't suitable.

FRED. Wear them in good health. (*HE exits.*)

(GILES pockets the packages, goes back to typing as LIBBY, drying her hair, enters from stairs.)

LIBBY. 'Morning.
GILES. Good morning.

(THEY smile at one another for a moment before SHE notices the flowers.)

LIBBY. Oh, where did the flowers come from?
GILES. The garden. They're—for you.

(Touched, SHE looks at him for a moment, picks up the flowers, smells them.)

LIBBY. They're beautiful, Giles.
GILES. Yes—well, I don't have much of a selection—it's mostly a vegetable garden, but—I thought you might like them as—well, sort of a memento.

(SHE is looking at him.)

GILES. Are you all right?

LIBBY. Yes. I'm just fighting off an attack of girlishness. (*Replacing flowers.*) Dangerous to do that sort of thing to someone my age. Causes heart palpitations.
GILES. Well, you gave me a few heart palpitations last night.
LIBBY. (*Blushing.*) Is it hot in here or is it just me?
GILES. (*Quickly.*) I'm sorry, I shouldn't have brought it up. I mean—I didn't mean to embarrass you—

LIBBY. No, that's okay—it's—okay. It's a novel sensation.

GILES. Yes—this is a very difficult stage.

LIBBY. What stage?

GILES. Well, I suppose one could call it the "never again" stage.

LIBBY. Never again?

GILES. Yes, where one knows that one will never experience certain things ever again.

LIBBY. Sex?

GILES. Well, possibly. I was thinking more of new friendships, dreams coming true, adventure.

LIBBY. Yeah—depressing, ain't it?

GILES. One comes to terms with it. That's what is so—unsettling about all this. When you walked in the house two nights ago, well, I was attracted to you. I am not romantic by nature. I always thought that sort of thing was—childish.

LIBBY. So is ice cream, but it still tastes good.

GILES. Perhaps—but I thought I'd closed the door on—all that—it took me by surprise. I'm not usually so rude, you know.

LIBBY. Is that why you said all those terrible things about the States?

(A slight pause.)

GILES. Partly. The fact is, it just knocked me for six and I didn't know how to behave.

LIBBY. Yeah, we're all under-rehearsed.

GILES. Under-rehearsed?

LIBBY. For this age. I mean who knew?

GILES. Knew what?

LIBBY. We'd live this long.

(THEY smile at one another for a moment.)

GILES. Yes—Well, you're looking very chipper, for someone who didn't get to bed until four o'clock.

LIBBY. Yeah. Haven't stayed up that late since I was in college. So that's what you work with—a typewriter.

GILES. What did you think—a quill pen?

LIBBY. Wouldn't be a bit surprised.

GILES. Do all Americans think we're behind the times?

LIBBY. Well, if they think about England at all it's, you know, as the land of remembrance.

GILES. And America?

LIBBY. The land of opportunity.

GILES. Of course. Where just about anybody can become President.

LIBBY. *(Grins.)* And, unfortunately, usually does. *(Heading for fireplace.)* Do you mind if I finish drying my hair in here?

GILES. Oh, you didn't take a shower?

LIBBY. Afraid so.

GILES. I should have warned you about that. There's very little pressure.

LIBBY. Now you tell me. Why don't you get it fixed?

GILES. It's not possible. *(As SHE looks at him.)* You see, it's on the second floor.

LIBBY. Ah, that explains it.

(HE watches her for a moment; SHE turns, notices him.)

LIBBY. What?

GILES. Oh—sorry. I haven't seen a woman dry her hair for—ages.

LIBBY. You never told me about your marriage.

GILES. It—ended—badly.

LIBBY. Don't they always?

GILES. It was—quite a while ago.

LIBBY. But you still don't like to talk about it?

GILES. There's nothing much to talk about.

(SHE waits.)

GILES. She just—left me.

LIBBY. Why?

GILES. It's not that interesting a subject.

LIBBY. It is to me.

GILES. *(Reluctantly.)* Ah. Well, in those days, I was still struggling. My first two books had been rejected and—we were going through a bad financial patch. It bothered her—not to be able to buy—things.

LIBBY. Yeah—so?

GILES. So she left me.

LIBBY. Just like that?

GILES. She met—another man.

LIBBY. *(Gently.)* That must have been painful.

GILES. Yes. I was—very fond of her. Well, of course.

LIBBY. You didn't see it coming at all?

GILES. No. I suppose I live—too much inside my head.

LIBBY. She must have been nuts.

GILES. *(Embarrassed.)* Thank you. I mean—thank you.

(HE gives a little shrug. Also slightly embarrassed, SHE turns away, continues brushing. HE watches her.)

GILES. Sometimes I wish I could be more like that.

LIBBY. Like what?

GILES. Well—er—uninhibited.

LIBBY. *(Stops brushing, looks at him. Puzzled.)* You've never brushed your hair in front of anyone?

GILES. No, I meant—direct, open.

LIBBY. You did pretty well last night.

GILES. I'm sorry about going on like that.

LIBBY. Why? I did my share of talking too. And *that's* a big surprise, huh?

GILES. Yes, but for me it was—highly unusual.

LIBBY. Talking?

GILES. Nattering on at great length like that. Probably the wine. No, it was you. I mean, I usually don't talk—about myself—or how I feel. I suppose my only excuse is that whenever I looked at you—you seemed to actually be interested.

LIBBY. Why wouldn't I be?

GILES. Well, you see, the fact is—most people find me boring.

(HE stands and we see that, instead of trousers, HE is wearing striped pajama bottoms. SHE doesn't react to this.)

LIBBY. *(Surprised.)* How do you know?

GILES. Oh, there are dozens of subtle signs. Mainly, the way their eyes glaze over when I'm talking.

LIBBY. You're not boring, Giles.

GILES. No?

LIBBY. No. You're eccentric.

GILES. Eccentric?

LIBBY. Yeah. And this might be a good time to tell you that you've forgotten to put your pants on.

GILES. (*Looks down, is embarrassed.*) Oh, not again!

LIBBY. (*Amused.*) Again?

GILES. The last time I drove all the way into London before I noticed. Well, actually, I *never* noticed. Someone else did.

LIBBY. Where was that?

GILES. In Harrod's Food Halls.

LIBBY. (*Laughs.*) Listen, kid, people who think they're boring, usually aren't.

GILES. Be that as it may, but— (*HE moves away, awkwardly.*) I don't really have anyone I can confide in— well, there's Fred, of course, but he's not—anyway, I'm afraid I rather got out of the habit and—the point is, I was perfectly happy with my life, but last night you made me realize it was lacking something.

LIBBY. What?

GILES. A friend. Look, I seem to be taking the scenic route here, but—oh, why do I have such trouble paying a compliment?

LIBBY. I don't know, but you've certainly caught my interest.

GILES. (*Blurting.*) It's not just sex!

(*SHE just stares at him.*)

GILES. Not that that wasn't excellent.

LIBBY. Honey, at this age, there's no such thing as *bad* sex. Just getting out of the starting block is worth a cheer.

GILES. Yes, well, look, I find you very attractive—well, of course—but you must hear that all the time.

LIBBY. Not really. Nobody's ever accused me of being sexy before. At least not in public.

GILES. Yes, well, I just wanted you to know that my feeling for you is not just physical—there's more to it than that. I'm sorry, I'm really not good at this.

LIBBY. (*Quietly.*) You're doing just fine.

GILES. Anyway, I wanted to thank you.

LIBBY. For what?

GILES. For being—for acting like—my friend.

(*SHE moves to him, puts her hand out to touch his cheek.*)

LIBBY. (*Gently.*) You're very—welcome.

(*THEY are looking at one another, as DAISY comes down the stairs and into the room.*)

DAISY. 'Morning, Mr. St. James.

GILES. Oh. Good morning, Daisy—and please, call me Giles.

DAISY. (*Notices typewriter.*) Well, will you just look at that antique machine. I tell you, everything over here is just so darned cute. You always work in your pajamas?

GILES. Uh—yes. Old superstition.

DAISY. Where's my buddy Fred?

GILES. I believe he's in the kitchen attending to his Spotted Dick.

(A pause.)

DAISY. Now you just made that up, didn't you?

GILES. Not at all. It's a pudding he's making for dinner tonight.

DAISY. Sugar, I'm not even going to ask about the ingredients.

FRED. *(Enters from kitchen.)* 'Morning, ladies. *(Moving to sideboard.)* I just need a screwdriver to attach the plug to the new toaster so we can have toast for breakfast.

GILES. I was thinking that Daisy might like to see the castle at Windsor.

FRED. *(Doubtfully.)* Well, that's a long drive. *(To Libby.)* You up to that, love?

LIBBY. No thanks, Fred. I think I'll stick around here—maybe take a long run.

FRED. Of course. Sorry about that. The thing about getting older is you're not too quick on the uptake anymore. Oh, Giles?

GILES. Yes?

FRED. Bit drafty, isn't it?

GILES. It is? Oh, see what you mean. No—it's fine.

FRED. *(Looking at screwdriver.)* I hope I remember how to do this.

LIBBY. You want me to give you a hand?

FRED. You know anything about British appliances?

LIBBY. Well, I'll give it a shot.

(As THEY head for door.)

FRED. I never was mechanical. I even have trouble working a light switch. Of course, give me a stuck zipper and I'm your man. Don't look at me like that—I was a dresser.

(THEY exit to kitchen.
DAISY watches him put typewriter away for a moment.)

DAISY. It's nice that you and Libby made up.

GILES. Good Lord, do you people tell each other everything?

DAISY. It's just girl talk, sugar.

GILES. How did you happen to end up working with her?

DAISY. I searched her out and practically tackled her around the knees.

GILES. Why?

DAISY. She's a genius.

GILES. Oh, come on now. Shakespeare was a genius, Beethoven, Michelangelo, Einstein perhaps. I hardly think a television producer is a genius.

DAISY. Oh, I don't mean she's like those guys. She's a genius at what she does.

GILES. What is that?

DAISY. She makes things happen.

GILES. Yes, I'm beginning to think that she does.

DAISY. She's good people, Giles. But right now she's a bit desperate and could use some help.

GILES. She never mentioned that.

DAISY. Yeah, well, that's her only fault. She's never asked anyone for help in her life.

LIBBY. (*Enters.*) I fixed it. Fred wants us all in the kitchen for breakfast.

(*DAISY exits.*)

GILES. Daisy has been telling me that she's a bit of an Anglophile.

LIBBY. Well, she's very young. (*As SHE turns to go.*) Oh, Fred said to bring in the paper.

(*As GILES moves to get it.*)

LIBBY. He said if he and Daisy are going on an outing, he wants to check the weather forecast.

GILES. (*Glancing at paper.*) I don't know why he bothers. It's always— (*HE stops in mid-stride, an unbelieving expression on his face.*) Oh, my God.

LIBBY. What is it?

GILES. I—I don't—believe—I can't—

LIBBY. Giles, are you okay? What in hell's the matter? (*SHE takes paper, reads.*) "Mystery Man Unmasked. It has been learned that the popular mystery writer, T.J. Walbourne, is in fact our own Giles St. James who has been living outside of—" (*SHE stops, looks up, baffled.*) How did they get this?

(*HE is staring at her.*)

LIBBY. Why are you staring at me like that?

GILES. (*Unbelievingly.*) Is this your idea of—of friendship?

LIBBY. What?

GILES. My God, how could you do such a thing!

LIBBY. Do what? Giles, I had nothing—

GILES. What sort of person are you? Who would behave so despicably? (*As SHE tries to speak.*) Do you know what you've done to me? You'll go to any lengths, won't you? Try money and if money doesn't work, try sex—and if that doesn't bring him around and he still insists on his privacy, then it's very simple—destroy it!

LIBBY. (*Moving to him.*) Giles—

GILES. Get the hell away from me! I should have trusted my instincts when I first laid eyes on you. You're just like all the rest of those—crass, insensitive, money-grubbing Americans who don't care who they trample in their pursuit of—

LIBBY. Giles, I don't know what the hell you're talking about!

GILES. Then let me put it in words you'll understand— let's "cut to the chase." I'm leaving and when I get back, I want you as far away from here as possible! (*HE exits through the front door, slamming it behind him.*)

(*Very shaken and hurt by his outburst, LIBBY stands motionless.*
FRED enters, followed by DAISY.)

FRED. What's going on? Who was that shouting? Was that Giles? He never shouts.

DAISY. (*Shocked.*) Libby, why—why are you crying?

LIBBY. I'm not!

DAISY. But—

LIBBY. I'm not! Look, we have to get packed.

DAISY. Where we going?

LIBBY. Home! *(SHE exits up the stairs.)*

(FRED looks at a nonplussed DAISY.)

FRED. And I thought we were all starting to speak the same language.

CURTAIN

END OF ACT I

ACT II

Scene 1

SCENE: Two days later. Midday.

The living room of Libby's second floor New York apartment in the East Village. In contrast to Giles' traditionally furnished house, the apartment is modern—what is often called "high-tech"—and is painted white with accents of vivid primary colors. The room contains a desk, a computer, sofa, chairs, large television set and a window overlooking the street.

The room also functions as Libby's office and the sparseness of the decor is offset by overflowing bookshelves which also house two rather tarnished Emmy awards, and a clutter of papers, manuscripts, magazines, telephone books, etc., which are piled on the desk and floor. There are some photos of Libby and her daughter, obviously taken some years ago, in evidence, along with some faded shots of Libby on the sets of various shows she has produced.

AT RISE: Before the curtain rises, we hear the SOUNDS OF NEW YORK—a cacophony of honking horns, squealing brakes and the siren of an ambulance or police car.

*As the LIGHTS COME UP, we find LIBBY looking at a
photo of her daughter. SHE hesitates, picks up phone
as, unobserved by her, DAISY, carrying some mail,
enters. SHE watches as LIBBY dials a long distance
number, hyperventilates slightly, waits a couple of
beats and abruptly hangs up.*

DAISY. Who you calling?
LIBBY. (*Startled.*) God, Daisy, when I get some money
I'm going to buy you something to wear that jangles.

*(DAISY moves to close window which almost shuts out
the NOISES of the city. During the following, SHE
opens mail and checks it.)*

DAISY. Were you phoning Giles?
LIBBY. Giles? Of course not—why would you think
that?
DAISY. It was long distance and you were
hyperventilating. It had to be Giles or your daughter.
LIBBY. It was Cindy.
DAISY. Why'd you hang up?
LIBBY. I decided I'm not ready.
DAISY. When will you be ready?
LIBBY. Right after I win the Nobel Prize. Anything in
the mail?
DAISY. Just more bills. Were you expecting
something?
LIBBY. Oh, I don't know. I always think, at the last
moment, the cavalry is going to ride in with flags flying
and trumpets blaring to save us all.

DAISY. (*Starts to attempt to clear up desk.*) So you're not going to phone her?

LIBBY. No, I've had enough rejection for one week. What are you doing?

DAISY. Trying to get this junk in some sort of order.

LIBBY. Leave it—I like it that way. Reminds me of my life.

DAISY. Something will show up, Libby. You're too talented to be out of work.

LIBBY. It doesn't work that way, kid.

DAISY. Talent doesn't count?

LIBBY. Not much when your head has ended up in as many soup bowls as mine has.

DAISY. But you're sober now, so why won't they give you a job?

LIBBY. It's not a business that hands out second chances easily—especially to a woman with a mouth on her like mine. The only way they're going to let me play in their sandbox again is if I have some leverage. That's why getting the rights to—oh, to hell with it, I can always get another job.

DAISY. As what?

LIBBY. (*Looking around messy room.*) Interior decorator.

DAISY. Yeah, I've been meaning to talk to you about your room.

LIBBY. When did you get cast as the mother? That's my part!

DAISY. And what's mine?

LIBBY. Loyal adopted daughter who, unfortunately, was raised by Carolina hillbillies and talks real weird. (*Notices DAISY studying her.*) What is it?

DAISY. I've never seen you so down before.

LIBBY. I thought I was being abnormally cheerful.

DAISY. Yeah, that's what I mean. You know your trouble?

LIBBY. I could write a book.

DAISY. Are you trying to pretend that you weren't affected by that whole experience with Giles?

LIBBY. (*Shrugging it off.*) It was just a physical—encounter. Doesn't mean a thing.

DAISY. Oh?

LIBBY. Listen, if someone accidentally touches me on the subway, I stay in love for twenty-four hours.

DAISY. Now what's that supposed to mean?

LIBBY. (*Shrugs.*) I guess I crave affection. Will you stop looking at me like that? What's so terrible? I had my first and last one-night stand. Makes me feel like a normal American.

DAISY. You don't want to talk about it.

LIBBY. Why would you say that?

DAISY. Because every time you don't want to talk about something you try for a cheap laugh.

LIBBY. There's no such thing. Some of the words that have escaped my mouth have cost me a lot. (*As DAISY looks at her.*) Look, it wouldn't have worked out, Daisy. We had absolutely nothing in common.

DAISY. What about chemistry?

LIBBY. At our age chemistry is less important than liking the same brand of dental adhesive.

DAISY. You're doing it again.

LIBBY. All right. For the past two days I've thought every country-western song was written specifically about me. I had high hopes and I was sorry it wasn't meant to be. But I'll recover. Satisfied, doctor?

DAISY. Look, how about this? I got my last unemployment check. You put on some coffee and I'll run down and get us a large prune Danish.

LIBBY. Sure—that's all I need, on top of everything—out of control thighs.

DAISY. Your blood sugar's low. You'll feel better after you put something rotten inside your body. (*SHE exits.*)

(LIBBY moves to pick up the photos of her children, looks at them pensively.
We hear LOUD ROCK AND ROLL MUSIC coming from upstairs. LIBBY replaces photos, automatically takes a broom and bangs it against the ceiling. The MUSIC SUBSIDES.)

LIBBY. Thank you, Leroy.

(The BUZZER SOUNDS. LIBBY moves to the intercom.)

LIBBY. Yeah?

(We hear DAISY GIVING THE IMITATION OF A TRUMPET.
LIBBY is puzzled by the sound, shrugs, finds two coffee mugs under the debris on the desk and is moving towards the kitchen when GILES, carrying suitcases and wearing an overcoat, sweating and with a wide-eyed, stricken look, enters.)

LIBBY. (*Stunned.*) My God, what are you doing here? Who let you in?

GILES. Daisy. Look, I could really use a drink.

LIBBY. What's the matter with you?

GILES. I just had the most terrifying experience of my life.

LIBBY. What?

GILES. I was driven here in a New York taxicab. It was filthy, the man drove like a—a demented person, he hit every pothole in the road, the cab had no shock absorbers and we kept bouncing in the air, totally out of touch with the ground.

LIBBY. You should have asked him to slow down.

GILES. I did, but he didn't understand me.

LIBBY. Yeah, well, you're going to have to learn to speak like the rest of us.

GILES. In Bangladesh? And he didn't know where anyplace was. Fred wanted to see Times Square, and he couldn't find it. Are they all like that? I mean, aren't they *trained*?

LIBBY. Where is Fred now?

GILES. He went off with Daisy to get a salt beef sandwich. That's all he's been nattering on about for the past two days—salt beef.

LIBBY. What are you doing here, Giles?

GILES. (*Awkwardly.*) Well, actually, I thought I needed to mend some broken fences with you.

LIBBY. So you flew all the way from England? Why didn't you phone?

GILES. Well, after the bit of a row we had, I didn't think you'd return my calls.

LIBBY. Americans return their phone calls.

GILES. (*Nonplussed.*) So do we.

LIBBY. I mean the same week.

GILES. You people are all in such a hurry. Look, do you mind if I take off my coat? (*HE does, revealing a tweed suit, notices her look.*) What is it?

LIBBY. I don't believe you're standing in my apartment in your grouse-hunting outfit.

GILES. It's my travelling suit. I wasn't sure of what the weather would be. It's absolutely sweltering out.

LIBBY. It's fifty-eight degrees.

GILES. That's what I mean. Is it me or is it warm in here? Do you have some sort of hot air blasting into the room?

LIBBY. It's the central heating.

GILES. Doesn't that dry out your sinuses?

LIBBY. What's so great about wet sinuses?

GILES. (*Looks at her for a moment.*) Look here, I can understand your being somewhat ticked off at me. I mean, I did state my case rather—firmly. That was quite unforgivable. Oh, not so much what I said but the way I said it.

LIBBY. At the top of your voice?

GILES. What? Yes—quite. I never yell.

LIBBY. But, in my case, you made an exception?

GILES. I was hurt.

LIBBY. Oh?

GILES. I thought you were my friend. I—I trusted you.

LIBBY. Two-way street.

GILES. Yes, well, I'm rather new at that.

LIBBY. Trusting people?

GILES. The point is, when Fred came back from driving you to the airport, he told me that it was Daisy, not you, who let the cat out of the bag at the newspaper office.

LIBBY. She didn't mean to. Without my knowing, she had gone to the paper and given them a personality profile and asked if they knew anyone in the area who fit it.

GILES. Rather irresponsible.

LIBBY. She's young. She makes mistakes.

GILES. Why didn't you tell me it wasn't you?

LIBBY. "Never explain, never apologize."

GILES. Is that another saying from one of your T-shirts?

LIBBY. Would you have listened?

GILES. Yes, well, anyway the phone hasn't stopped ringing since you left, and yesterday there was actually a band of journalists camped outside my door. Absolute hooligans!

LIBBY. Hooligans?

GILES. They trampled all over my marrow beds. They've quite ruined my garden, you know. That's one of the reasons I decided to escape and come here.

LIBBY. What are the others?

GILES. Well—look, do you mind if I sit?

(SHE goes to remove some manuscripts from a chair as HE looks around.)

GILES. Are you moving?

LIBBY. No, I'm just messy.

GILES. Is your char on holiday?

LIBBY. No, I can't afford a cleaning woman.

GILES. Yes, that's the other thing. You see, I assumed you were this rich American who thought she could get anything by just waving her cheque book.

LIBBY. I thought you'd be more likely to trust me with the rights if you thought I was rich and powerful.

GILES. But you said you bribed someone. If you didn't have any money, how could you do that?

LIBBY. I offered them points—a small percentage in the series—should I land the rights.

GILES. (*Looks at her for a moment.*) My God, you were really desperate, weren't you?

LIBBY. Yes.

GILES. But why?

LIBBY. (*Simply.*) I felt I was getting old and nobody wanted me anymore.

GILES. (*Touched by her admission.*) Ah—yes, I see.

LIBBY. Do you?

GILES. I'm not entirely insensitive to the terrors of being discarded.

(*SHE doesn't say anything. Somewhat embarrassed, HE moves away and lights cigarette.*)

GILES. Anyway, when Fred told me that Daisy had confided that you were up against it and needed the money to get on your feet again so that you could get your children back, I felt like— (*HE stops as he sees HER waving her arms to clear the smoke.*) Oh, sorry, I forgot. Where shall I put this?

(*SHE takes cigarette, stubs it out in a mug.*)

GILES. Anyway, that's why I dropped by to apologize.

LIBBY. Excuse me—I'm confused. This past conversation—was that you apologizing?

GILES. Of course. What did you think I was doing?

LIBBY. Hard to tell.

GILES. Not everything has to be *stated*, Libby.

LIBBY. No, not everything.

GILES. All right, dammit! I'm sorry! (*HE moves to window, looks out.*) Do you have these bars on the window to keep people from falling out?

LIBBY. No, to keep people from falling in. (*HE turns to look at her.*) Goes with the territory with a second-story apartment.

GILES. Really?

LIBBY. But we have terrific water pressure. Where are you staying?

GILES. We don't know yet. I suppose we'll look around for some sort of bed and breakfast place.

LIBBY. You've got to be kidding.

GILES. You don't have them here?

LIBBY. Yes, there's one down the street with seven hundred rooms. It's called a hotel. This is New York, Giles.

GILES. Well, be that as it may, one doesn't have a lot of money to recklessly sling around. Anyway, I've heard about those hotels. The windows won't open.

LIBBY. How long are you planning on staying?

GILES. Well, that depends on how long it takes.

LIBBY. Takes to do what?

GILES. Get this thing rolling.

LIBBY. What thing?

GILES. You know, for someone usually so quick-witted, sometimes you're quite obtuse. (*As SHE stares at him.*) This television thing you're so keen to do.

LIBBY. Do you mean you're willing to give me the rights?

GILES. Libby, haven't I already said that, in so many words?

LIBBY. (*Weakly.*) Not in so many words.

GILES. Why on earth do you think I'm here?

LIBBY. My God, it's true. Sometimes the Cavalry does arrive in the nick of time!

GILES. I don't quite follow you.

LIBBY. (*Very elated.*) It doesn't matter. Giles, I could kiss you!

GILES. (*Nervously.*) Yes, well, I wouldn't do that, if I were you. (*As SHE looks at him.*) This Harris tweed emits an odd smell when damp.

LIBBY. (*Evenly.*) You just talked me out of it.

GILES. It's nothing personal.

LIBBY. Oh, good.

GILES. Now look here, for the past two days I've been hounded and harassed in my own house, and then I've been transported three thousand miles away to a noisy city that, quite frankly, makes my sphincter extremely clenched. I am about to embark upon a task for which it's possible I am entirely inadequate, so I'm completely at sixes and sevens and I feel the only way I'll be able to cope at all is by staying in a detached, calm state. I am not good at change. I mean, any untoward—event and I'm liable to go off half-cocked. Do you understand?

LIBBY. Does this mean that nobody in this room is going to get laid then?

GILES. I—beg your pardon?

LIBBY. I'm sorry—you bring out the worst in me.

GILES. Oh?

LIBBY. I tend to say outrageous things just to get a visible reaction. My analyst was working on that when I had to quit.

GILES. You've been in psychoanalysis?

LIBBY. Yeah, I know—if I'm like this now, what was I like *before* therapy.

GILES. No, it's not that. It's just that I don't know anyone who's been in analysis.

LIBBY. I don't know anyone who hasn't. So—what happens now?

GILES. Well, I've alerted my agent that your agent might be calling.

LIBBY. I don't have an agent.

GILES. No?

LIBBY. I know how to make a deal.

GILES. (*Dryly.*) I'm sure you do.

LIBBY. Look, would you accept a firm handshake?

GILES. What? Oh, yes, of course.

(*HE takes her proffered hand and, rather awkwardly, THEY shake hands. Whether this would lead to anything else, we don't know, as DAISY and FRED, carrying deli sandwiches in aluminum foil, enter.*)

DAISY. Hi, how you doing, Giles?

GILES. Oh, hello, Daisy.

(*FRED moves to give LIBBY a hug.*)

FRED. How are you, love?

DAISY. We brought you some pastrami sandwiches. (*SHE clears spot on table, unwraps sandwiches through following.*) So, what do you think of our fair city? Be great when they finish it, huh?

GILES. Finish it? Oh, yes, there does seem to be a lot of construction.

DAISY. Yeah, New York has always been sort of like a work in progress.

GILES. Ah.

DAISY. (*Handing him sandwich.*) Here, dive in.

GILES. My God, one would have to be a crocodile to eat this.

DAISY. Just watch Fred.

FRED. Tastes exactly like I remembered.

LIBBY. I guess New York has changed since you were here, Fred.

FRED. Well, everything has, love. Even me. But the people haven't. They're still as friendly as ever.

LIBBY. (*Dubiously.*) New Yorkers, friendly?

FRED. You just have to give them half a chance. When Daisy was in the shop, I started talking to a young chap and he couldn't have been nicer.

DAISY. That was a crack dealer, Fred.

FRED. Crack?

LIBBY. Drugs. So you be careful and remember that this is not 1948. You learn quickly not to make eye contact in this city because it's filled with people who either want your money, your soul or your body.

FRED. Well, the last one doesn't seem too bad a deal. (*Noticing TV set.*) Will you look at the size of this. How many channels does it have?

DAISY. About fifty.

FRED. Oh, lovely. Did you say fifty?

DAISY. (*Hands him earphones and a remote control.*) Or sixty. Don't get too excited—you still can't find anything worth watching.

(SHE flips on set [we can't see screen] and smiles as she watches FRED, who has put on headphones and is gazing at the set, a happy smile on his face.)

DAISY. I think we've just lost Fred to sex and violence.

LIBBY. (*To Giles.*) You'd better watch out for young "Candide" here. If he wanders into the wrong neighborhood, he's liable to get a gun stuck in his ear.

GILES. Guns are really that prevalent?

LIBBY. It's in the Constitution. The right to bear arms—and buy them at the supermarket. Goes back to 1788.

GILES. Yes, well, I have no objection to anyone owning a musket. I just draw the line at Uzi's.

DAISY. My granddaddy has a bumper sticker that says "Guns don't kill people. People kill people."

GILES. No. People with guns kill people.

DAISY. Well, how about that? You and Libby finally agree on something.

GILES. Well, I agree with you about the taste of this sandwich. It's—jolly interesting.

LIBBY. We probably agree on more subjects than you'd think.

DAISY. Is that why you looked as if you were both about to consummate something when we walked in?

GILES. I beg your pardon? Oh yes, I see what you mean.

LIBBY. Giles has agreed to let us have the rights, Daisy.

DAISY. Oh, wow, that's just terrific! (*SHE hugs Libby.*) I told you something would turn up! Congratulations! (*SHE hugs a somewhat disconcerted GILES.*) You, too, Giles! When do we start?

LIBBY. Well, first of all, we have to devise a plan.

GILES. A plan for what?

LIBBY. How we're going to pitch this thing to the network.

GILES. Pitch?

LIBBY. Make an oral presentation.

GILES. I thought it was all settled. Do you mean I have to *audition*?

LIBBY. Everybody does.

GILES. But I'm a writer. Why should I have to *talk* about my work? (*As SHE goes to speak.*) No, I really can't do that.

LIBBY. You won't have to. You'll just be there to give the project authenticity.

GILES. How will I do that?

LIBBY. Just sit there in your funny suit and occasionally say something with an English accent. They associate British accents with—culture. It intimidates them, which will give us an edge. Look, I'm sure they'll go for it—the pitch is just a formality that network executives like to schedule to fill their days and make them feel they're being creative.

GILES. Where will this ritual take place?

LIBBY. Probably in L.A.

GILES. Won't the fare be exorbitant? We're on a very strict budget, you know.

LIBBY. They'll pay our way out there. I'll try and set it up for next week. That'll give us time to write the outlines.

GILES. Look, I'm sorry if I seem dense, but why do we have to write outlines? After all, the books are already written.

LIBBY. People won't read out there.

GILES. Won't or can't?

LIBBY. It's a moot point. Anyway, that's why they employ readers who synopsize the material into a couple of paragraphs. But even if they do get around to reading the synopsis, they have trouble visualizing how it will look on film.

GILES. But isn't that their job?

LIBBY. Their job is to get ratings and protect their ass. You see, most of the people in charge of creative affairs graduated from business schools, so they don't know much about show business.

GILES. None of them have creative backgrounds?

LIBBY. Well, maybe the odd hairdresser. I thought we'd pitch the three books that are the most "high concept."

GILES. High concept?

LIBBY. Can be described in one sentence.

GILES. You mean I wasted two hundred and seventy-five pages?

LIBBY. Don't start getting sensitive on me, Giles. Of course we'll have to do a scene by scene breakdown on all three.

GILES. Sounds like an awful lot of work to get done in a week.

LIBBY. No sweat. We can start tonight.

GILES. Yes, well, we'd better find some lodging.

LIBBY. You can stay here. Come on, I'll get you settled.

(SHE moves to touch FRED, who has been raptly watching TV, on the shoulder. HE takes off headphones.)

FRED. (*Happily.*) I just watched fourteen advertisements in a row. Fourteen . . .

DAISY. Yeah, some people think America is all about going shopping.

FRED. In between the advertisements, there was this show where they took this whole family and did—what did they call it—a makeover.

GILES. Makeover?

FRED. Yes, you see them before and then they take them away and put them in new clothes with different hairdos. It was quite interesting. I wish they'd left the children alone though. I don't know, I always thought kids were beautiful just as they are. They also made over the dog.

GILES. Come on, Fred, Libby's kindly invited us to stay here.

FRED. Well, bless her heart. (*To Giles.*) I told you so.

(This really embarrasses GILES.)

GILES. One really can't take him anywhere.

FRED. (*Moves to get suitcase.*) Which way then?

DAISY. Down the hall, Fred.

LIBBY. Just don't expect Buckingham Palace.

FRED. I've stayed in Buckingham Palace, love, and it's nothing to write home about.

DAISY. Fred, you're full of surprises. How did that happen?

FRED. I once had a friend who was in the Coldstream Guards.

(THEY exit.)

LIBBY. I'll put you in my room.

GILES. But where will you sleep?

LIBBY. Out here on the couch.

GILES. Oh no, I couldn't possibly take your room.

LIBBY. I won't charge you any more.

GILES. No, it's not that.

LIBBY. I *know* it's not that. I was making a joke.

GILES. Oh. Anyway, I wouldn't feel comfortable taking your bed.

LIBBY. Look, we'll both be more comfortable. I'm an insomniac and I like to be free to pad around during the night, make myself a cup of coffee, jot down ideas, replay the tapes of my misguided life.

GILES. I've learned that one shouldn't dwell on the past.

LIBBY. Easily said.

GILES. I know.

LIBBY. (*Looks at him for a moment.*) Hey, do you mind if I say something?

GILES. (*Uncomfortably.*) It's not going to be— intensely personal, is it?

LIBBY. I appreciate your trusting me this way.

GILES. What way?

LIBBY. With your life's work. And I want you to know I'll do my best to justify your faith in me. (*A beat.*) Yeah, I know, there I go stating things again. At least I didn't hug you.

GILES. Is that a joke?

LIBBY. Sort of.

GILES. (*Breaks eye contact, moves away, turns.*) Look here, I hope you weren't offended by my little speech earlier. I just think it could be uncomfortable unless we— uh—we—

LIBBY. Keep our hands off each other.

GILES. Yes. (*Quickly.*) Not, of course, that I would presume to think that you—but, well, we're very different—sorts of people and we tend to—to disagree on many things, which will make our partnership difficult enough, and it would be even more unless we—uh, am I making myself clear?

LIBBY. Absolutely.

GILES. Good.

(*HE picks up a suitcase and a briefcase which, on his way to the door, falls open and spills about forty-eight condoms on the floor.*
HE doesn't notice, but LIBBY does.)

LIBBY. Giles? (*HE turns.*) You dropped something.

(*HE now sees condoms.*)

GILES. Oh, my God.

LIBBY. Was there a sale?

(Completely embarrassed, HE gets down on his hands and knees during following.)

GILES. I'm—I'm terribly sorry. They're not mine. That is, Fred—packs for me.

LIBBY. *(Trying not to laugh.)* He must have a very high opinion of you.

GILES. *(Earnestly.)* Yes, well, Fred's always been a bit of an optimist. I mean, he tends to—to hero worship me.

LIBBY. Yeah, he really must because getting me pregnant would be some trick.

GILES. *(Still trying to pick up the condoms.)* No, he just thought I couldn't be too careful. Said one never knew where you'd been. *(Mortified.)* Oh God, that sounds awful! I hope you're not offended.

LIBBY. Nicest thing anybody's said about me in years.

(GILES fumbles with suitcase which opens again revealing a bunch of flowers.)

LIBBY. What are they?

GILES. Runiculas.

LIBBY. In your suitcase?

GILES. I smuggled them in—one is not supposed to bring in plants and—well, you seemed to like them and well, I thought I might need—a peace offering.

LIBBY. What a great combination. Runiculas and a gross of condoms. Giles, you certainly know the way to a girl's heart!

(SHE bursts out laughing.

HE stares at her.)

GILES. You think this is funny?

(Unable to speak through her laughter, SHE nods.)

GILES. I'll *never* understand you people.

(HE regards her soberly, as SHE continues to laugh and the CURTAIN FALLS.)

End of ACT II, Scene 1

ACT II

Scene 2

SCENE: Some ten days later.

AT RISE: We see the apartment is much tidier than before. There is a celebratory cake on the table, along with some plates and forks. DAISY is finishing tacking up a homemade banner reading "Welcome Home Giles and Libby." SHE moves to unroll some paper and extract two small flags—a Union Jack and a Stars and Stripes—on eighteen-inch sticks. The PHONE RINGS and, still holding the two flags, SHE picks it up.

DAISY. (*Into phone.*) Libby Daniels Productions—No, Giles is not here right now, but I'm expecting him any moment. May I say who called?—(*Slightly puzzled.*) Oh, okay. (*SHE hangs up, moves to deposit the two flags in a vase under the banner, and then exits to the kitchen.*)

(*GILES APPEARS in doorway. HE is holding a suitcase and looking grim. HE stands still for a moment, and then starts leaping around the room as he did in Act I, Scene 2.*)

GILES. Damn, damn, damn, damn, damn, damn, damn!!!

(*HE stops as HE sees DAISY who has been brought to the kitchen door by his noise and has been watching his gyrations with a puzzled expression.*)

DAISY. What's the matter, Giles? Did you have a bad taxi ride again?

(*HE shakes his head.*)

DAISY. What then? Is it the scripts?
GILES. They want to—(*HE has trouble saying it.*)—*Americanize* them!!

(*HE marches off into the bedroom as FRED, carrying luggage and some packages, enters.*)

FRED. Hello, love. (*HE deposits luggage, hugs her, looks at cake.*) Well, will you look at this!

DAISY. Where's Libby?

FRED. Oh, we took different flights. For some reason, Giles wanted to leave earlier.

DAISY. What's it like out there, Fred?

FRED. Oh, it's tacky, glitzy and vulgar—everything I've ever wanted. To tell the truth, a lot of it is very beautiful—lovely scenery, sunny skies, fancy cars—all goes down a treat. (*HE has taken off raincoat to reveal a T-shirt with the slogan "But What I Really Want To Do Is Direct" on it.*) What do you think?

DAISY. Definitely "you."

FRED. Got something for you, too. (*Extracting one from paper bag and giving it to her.*) Here you go, love. (*Pointing at logo of Beverly Hills Hotel.*) That's where we stayed. *Very* posh.

DAISY. Oh thanks, Fred. I love it! (*As SHE puts shirt on.*) So what did you do out there?

FRED. Well, I spent most of my time around the pool sucking in.

DAISY. (*Cutting cake.*) Sucking in?

FRED. Well, the place is filled with flat stomachs and beautiful people, isn't it? Everywhere you go—all these fit, tanned bodies and regular features and straight teeth.

DAISY. No homely people out there?

FRED. Only the writers. That's how you can tell they're writers—their faces are sort of pale and creased. (*HE takes cake from her.*) Thanks, dear.

DAISY. (*Shoots a glance at the bedroom*) Fred, was there any—uh—sexual tension out there?

FRED. Oh, probably. They have everything in L.A. Nothing that involved me, of course.

DAISY. I meant with Libby and Giles.

FRED. Oh, see what you mean. No, not so's you'd notice. I mean, I don't think they got around to doing each other the kindness or anything. Well, it was all business, wasn't it? Pity though—I had high hopes.

(GILES enters from the bedroom. HE has two small bottles of liquor in his hands. HE has had one or two drinks.)

GILES. *(Holding up bottle.)* Anyone like a drink?

FRED. Well, I wouldn't say "no." *(As GILES moves to pour.)* Where'd you get that then?

GILES. The plane. Squirrelled them away when the attendants weren't looking.

FRED. Giles believes in getting his money's worth.

GILES. Daisy?

DAISY. Why the hell not. *(As HE pours one for her.)* By the way, I thought your interview on "Entertainment Tonight" was just great.

GILES. *(Embarrassed.)* Libby talked me into it. Said I needed a "higher profile," whatever that means. Said it would give us more "clout." When she's in Hollywood, she really talks like that. Cheers.

FRED. *(Downs his drink.)* Well, I'd better unpack.

GILES. Don't unpack everything, Fred. Just the essentials.

FRED. *(After a slight beat.)* Whatever you say, guv. *(HE exits.)*

DAISY. Fred's been telling me all about his adventures in Hollywood.

GILES. Yes, well, Fred's impression and mine were quite dissimilar.

DAISY. You didn't have a good time?

GILES. (*Moves to replenish his drink.*) Our first encounter with the enemy was at what they call a "breakfast meeting." They really are so busy and important, they would never think of taking time simply to eat. We arrived first, and when these two obscenely young "movers and shakers" entered, my first thought was "My God, they're still teething." They carried phones—God forbid they should miss a call about a sick show they had to save right this minute. It got worse. In talking about one of the characters, I likened him to Richard III. They looked blank. I gently prodded their memories. Shakespeare. They just munched on their granola. I said, "Surely, you must of seen 'Richard III'?" One of them said "No, I don't go to see sequels." (*HE drinks, puts glass down.*) I was reduced to plunging into my totally inadequate imitation of Laurence Olivier. (*HE makes his hand crippled and does a creditable impression of Olivier.*) "Now is the winter of our discontent—" One of them allowed that he might have seen Richard III selling cameras on television when he was a child. The others thought I was talking about Emma Thompson's husband.

DAISY. You're making this up.

GILES. Not at all. For some reason this didn't bother Libby as much as it did me.

DAISY. She was probably trying to finesse the situation.

GILES. Oh, is that your word for it?

DAISY. What's yours?

GILES. Treason.

DAISY. Treason? Didn't that used to be a hanging offense, sir?

GILES. Sometimes the old ways were the best. Anyway, after cooling our heels for some days, we were summoned to attend a summit meeting with no less than twelve network executives. Libby and I were the only ones in the room who knew that World War II was *not* a sequel. Or perhaps it was. Anyway, that's when they made their creative suggestions.

DAISY. Which were?

GILES. (*Sighs.*) Their first idea was that I take my leading character; who, as you know, is a sixty-six-year-old retired Scotland Yard superintendent whose hobby is raising vegetables, and rewrite it for someone called Whoopie Goldberg. Well, even Libby, who was behaving like Chamberlain at Munich, raised her eyebrows at this, so they dropped it. All their other suggestions were to remove any subtlety, wit, intelligence or uniqueness from the scripts. I learned that, in their parlance, this is called "dumbing down a script."

DAISY. Did they want any other changes?

GILES. They want us to switch all our locales from a series of English villages to Hollywood. That's when I thought "Oh, stuff this for a lark" and walked out. (*HE pours himself another drink.*)

DAISY. What did you say to them?

GILES. Well, nothing. I just excused myself to get some water and never went back.

DAISY. Yeah, that's telling them.

GILES. I dislike confrontations.

DAISY. Sugar, that might be hard to avoid when Libby gets here.

GILES. (*Angrily.*) Oh, who gives a flying—(*Catches himself.*)—fig.

DAISY. How did Libby take your leaving?

GILES. I suspect she thinks I have trouble expressing my emotions.

DAISY. You suspect?

GILES. I never asked her. I went back to the hotel, collected Fred and went to the airport.

DAISY. But I thought you and Libby were friends.

GILES. I'm afraid that that is a fiction that doesn't work anymore.

(LIBBY, carrying suitcases and looking somewhat harassed, enters.)

DAISY. How you doing? (*SHE hugs her.*) You look beat.

LIBBY. I am. But I'm feeling better now. (*To Giles.*) Do you always run for the hills when you feel threatened?

GILES. You didn't need me to help with my own autopsy.

LIBBY. I can't believe you did that! Daisy, would you make me some tea—maybe throw a sandwich together? I'm starved.

DAISY. You got it. (*SHE exits to kitchen.*)

LIBBY. We can win this one yet, Giles. I flew in with a woman from Creative Affairs, Betsy Parker.

GILES. Why do Americans all have an "ie" or a "y" at the end of their names? Even when someone is christened Kim, they call her Kimmie.

LIBBY. Are you drunk?

GILES. No. Trying hard.

LIBBY. Look, I'm hot and I'm on edge and I'm not too thrilled with you right now, but let's put aside our personal differences for now and try and concentrate, Giles. This is important. They've agreed to make some trade-offs. They're willing to let us keep the character as written, but instead of him being sixty-six, they want him to be fifty-seven. They really wanted him to be fifty-one, but I negotiated them up to fifty-seven.

GILES. Why this obsession with his age?

LIBBY. Demographics, and they want him to still be open to sexual involvement.

GILES. There's a cut-off after fifty-seven? My God, they should have told us. We could have killed ourselves!

LIBBY. There's no "cut-off," but the opportunities are less—plentiful. Anyway, we're talking about a TV show, not life. Now they won't budge from wanting the locales changed to America. It's doable, Giles. The inspector can be visiting his grandchild in the States and—

GILES. Look, I don't want to hear any more!

LIBBY. Why not?

GILES. None of that is possible.

LIBBY. Everything is possible, Giles.

GILES. In "Concerto For Murder," a man is pushed into an old country well and the murderer plays Bartok's "Concerto For Orchestra" very loudly in his garden to cover the dying screams. I didn't come across many wells in Beverly Hills.

LIBBY. We'll use a jacuzzi.

GILES. A what?

LIBBY. A jacuzzi with a sliding top. Now they think classical music is a turn-off, so they suggest going with a specially written rap song.

GILES. (*Takes out a cigarette, stares at her.*) You can't be serious. Bloody hell—you can't be serious!!

LIBBY. I tried to talk them out of it, but— (*SHE stops.*) Bloody hell?

GILES. Yes—and sod on it too. Just—sod it! (*HE lights cigarette.*)

LIBBY. When did you start smoking again?

GILES. I never stopped. It's just that, in California, I pretended to stop to avoid the withering looks.

LIBBY. Well, I wish you'd stop now.

GILES. Don't drink, don't smoke, don't eat anything with any taste. You know, in about thirty years, you're going to be really sorry.

LIBBY. Why?

GILES. Because you're going to be in some hospital dying of *nothing*.

LIBBY. Hey, Giles, I know how you feel—I really do, but look at it this way. The books already exist—they'll always be there—but do you really want to keep doing the same thing over and over—the same way?

GILES. Of course I do.

LIBBY. Why?

GILES. Because that's what I know how to do! I don't know how to do it any other way!

LIBBY. You don't think the books might appear a trifle—uh—old-fashioned?

GILES. What's wrong with old-fashioned?

LIBBY. But this is a different medium—it requires new approaches.

GILES. Yes, well, I'm not as enamored with the new as you. Plastic is new, pollution is new, overpopulation, AIDS, rap music—they're all new.

LIBBY. Giles, it might just be fun to do this.

GILES. Going into a room and deliberately vulgarizing my work at the behest of some network—accountants—is your idea of fun?

LIBBY. Look, you think I don't know the system stinks? You think I don't know it produces lousy shows?

GILES. Then why do you have anything to do with it?

LIBBY. Because that's the *reality*! We can *win* this one, Giles—I just know we can.

GILES. What is so wonderful about winning?

LIBBY. We're talking about very big bucks here!

GILES. Ah, now we come to what it always comes down to. Money!

LIBBY. Makes the world go round.

GILES. Not my world.

LIBBY. You're full of shit, Giles.

GILES. We're not obsessed with money the way you are.

LIBBY. Oh yes you are! The British care like hell about it. You just don't want to *seem* as if you care about money. It's like the myth that they don't care about winning. They just hate to appear as if they're *trying*. It has to look easy. For God's sake, don't let anybody see you sweat! And that's why you haven't had a world class anything in decades! Well, let me tell you something—you don't get anything here by running away. You have to stay and maybe get your nose bloodied a bit. But the rewards are worth it.

GILES. For you perhaps—not for me! The price is too high!

LIBBY. What *price*?

GILES. I'm not going to sell out my principles just to help feed this country's insatiable lust for the mediocre. I am not blessed with a blinding talent. Not even close to the best in my rather limited field. I'm—competent—

(HE holds up his hand as SHE goes to speak.)

GILES. No, no—just hang on a minute! I'm just a chap with a knack for dreaming up puzzles and ways to solve them. This, along with a skill for inventing characters and dialogue, seem to have given my readers some pleasure and provided me with a decent livelihood. The point is, I'm totally aware of my limitations. But, despite this, my work is terribly, terribly important to me. Do you know why? Because it's the one thing in my life that is all mine! Nobody can take it away and that's of enormous comfort, and to lose it would be like cutting off a limb. And no amount of money could replace that.

LIBBY. *(Looks at him for a moment.)* No, it's something more.

GILES. More? There is no more.

LIBBY. You're mad about something else. You started acting weird when we were out there.

GILES. Everyone acts "weird" out there.

LIBBY. This has got nothing to do with "out there," does it? It's something to do with me, isn't it? Was it something I did? Was it?

GILES. Yes.

LIBBY. It was that bad?

GILES. Yes.

LIBBY. What, for Pete's sake? My God, you're half-crocked and I still have to put bamboo shoots under your fingernails to get an answer! Will you tell me? Are you mad because I didn't spend much time with you?

GILES. I really don't want to discuss it.

LIBBY. I could never find you. Why were you avoiding me?

GILES. Why are you acting so angry?

LIBBY. I'm acting angry because I'm angry! When I'm sad I cry, when I'm happy I laugh, and when I'm frustrated I act frustrated! (*SHE stops.*) My God, I sound just like Zorba The Greek! Look, sometimes why can't you just let go and behave like a human being?

GILES. (*Stung.*) Because every time I do I get kicked in the stomach!

LIBBY. Who by?

GILES. You! Every time I—I let my guard down, you start behaving like—like an American!

LIBBY. What do you mean?

(*HE doesn't answer.*)

LIBBY. Look, are you going to tell me, or is this another "That's for me to know and you to find out" deal?

GILES. (*Finally loses control*) All right, dammit! A week ago you thanked me for trusting you with my work and said you would do your best to justify my faith in you. You seemed sincere and I believed you. Perhaps because I *wanted* to believe you. Then when we got to Hollywood I was forced to sit by while you sold me out at every turn. I had to watch while those idiotic, know-nothing, illiterate network people made their ridiculous suggestions, and you sat with an inane smile on your face nodding your head as if they were making sense!

LIBBY. It's only a show, Giles.

GILES. Do you think I cared about the stupid show? I cared about you! Us! I thought that, despite our different nationalities, our differences were superficial and that there were certain shared fundamental values we could build on. But, as I watched your desperate maneuvering, I realized we didn't think the same way about anything and that we could never be friends. And it pains me. It pains me deeply! (*A beat.*) I'm sorry, I didn't mean to sound so emotional. Probably the liquor. Matter of fact, I'm feeling a bit legless. I think I'll walk around the block to get some air. (*HE moves slightly unsteadily to the door and exits.*)

(*LIBBY, very upset, moves to look out of window. FRED enters from bedroom.*)

FRED. His nibs gone out then?

(*SHE nods.*)

FRED. Perhaps I should keep him company. He seemed a bit het up.
LIBBY. Yeah, probably.
FRED. Well, keep your pecker up, love.
LIBBY. (*Turns to look at him.*) I'll do my best.
FRED. Ta, ta then. Won't be long. (*HE exits.*)

(*LIBBY automatically starts to clean up, but stops as SHE realizes SHE is holding a half-full bottle of the liquor Giles has left. SHE looks at it with a pensive expression. DAISY, unobserved, enters from kitchen with tea and a sandwich on a tray. SHE watches Libby for a moment.*)

DAISY. Don't you think you should pour that down the sink?

LIBBY. You don't have to worry about that, honey; but just don't leave any sharp instruments lying around. (*SHE puts tray on table.*)

DAISY. Oh, I wouldn't even think about that. Don't you know that committing suicide is probably the most self-destructive thing you can do.

LIBBY. Probably?

DAISY. Sugar, you're very inventive in that area. I couldn't help hear you yelling. What happened between you two out there?

LIBBY. (*Flatly.*) I sold him out.

DAISY. Why'd you do that?

LIBBY. Sometimes life gets complicated.

DAISY. Why were *you* so angry?

LIBBY. Because I sold him out.

DAISY. I don't know about the show, Lib. Maybe you're rocking a dead baby.

LIBBY. Is that some weird Southern expression?

DAISY. So what are you going to do?

LIBBY. Same as always. Keep talking.

DAISY. Just make sure you say the right words. How you really feel about him.

LIBBY. Are you kidding?

DAISY. Just thought I'd take a shot. (*DAISY puts two thumbs up and exits.*)

(*LIBBY wearily starts to take off her clothes. The PHONE RINGS.*)

LIBBY. (*Into phone.*) Hello—No, Giles is not here right now but—

(*We hear the LOUD MUSIC from the room above.*)

LIBBY. —he should be back soon—Yeah, he's staying here but—Look, will you hold on a minute? (*SHE puts phone down, bangs on the ceiling with the broom handle until the MUSIC subsides. SHE picks up phone again.*) Sorry—Look, can I tell him who's calling? (*Very surprised.*) His what?—Yeah, I will. You want to leave a number and—Yeah, I'll tell him.

(*Quite nonplussed, SHE hangs up, stands for a moment, absorbing the information she's just heard, then resumes taking off her clothes. SHE stops as SHE hears the BANGING of someone coming up the stairs.*
The door opens to reveal GILES, with a limp FRED over his shoulder.
GILES has blood all over him, He's out of breath, disheveled and is totally distraught. We will see that FRED has been hit on the head and is also bleeding. The following happens very fast, in a disorganized fashion.)

LIBBY. My God. What—what happened? What—
GILES. I think the bastards have killed Fred.
LIBBY. Here, put him on the—
GILES. (*Screaming.*) No, get something to wrap—

(*HE sinks to the floor as LIBBY grabs the tablecloth.*)

GILES. —he's still bleeding—oh my God, he's unconscious—he may not be— (*As SHE moves to treat the wound.*) No, I'll do that! Get an ambulance!—Phone— (*LIBBY is dialing.*)—get them here!

LIBBY. (*Into phone.*) Hello, this is an emergency—A man is hurt badly and—yes, right. (*SHE takes a breath.*) Forty-four East 9th Street. One flight up—Yes, yes, I will—Look, just get here!! (*SHE hangs up, turns towards Giles.*) They're on their way. They should—

(*SHE stops because of what SHE sees.*
GILES has Fred's head cradled in his lap and tears are streaming down his face. SHE gets a blanket from the back of the sofa, moves to put it over Fred, crouches down beside them.)

GILES. Keep away from him! Let me do it!
LIBBY. I was just going to—
GILES. Haven't you done enough damage?
LIBBY. (*Nonplussed.*) What?
GILES. You're the reason we're here! This wouldn't have happened if you hadn't disrupted our lives and just let us stay where we belonged! Just—let us alone!

(*Stunned by his outburst, SHE watches as GILES puts the blanket around the unconscious FRED.*)

CURTAIN

End of ACT 2, Scene 2

ACT II

Scene 3

Six a.m. the next morning.

*AT RISE: A very tired looking LIBBY and a shaky
GILES, a Band-Aid on his forehead, enter. SHE flicks
on a LIGHT. HE moves to sofa, slumps onto it.*

LIBBY. How's your head?
GILES. Still numb.

*(SHE moves to pick up sandwich Daisy had made,
examines it, finds it is dry, puts it aside.)*

LIBBY. You want something to eat? I could send out.
GILES. No, I wouldn't be able to keep anything down.
LIBBY. He'll be okay, Giles.
GILES. Then why are they keeping him at the hospital?
LIBBY. They just want to make sure he doesn't have a
concussion.
GILES. Bastards! How can anyone behave that way?
LIBBY. You never told me exactly what happened.
GILES. *(Wearily.)* Three men accosted me and wanted
my wallet. One stuck a gun in my ribs. That's when Fred
came along the street—he was confused about what was
happening and said, "Hey, what's going on then?" The man
took the gun out of my ribs and put it at Fred's throat.
That's when I dived at him. I don't remember much after

that except when I came to, Fred was still unconscious with his face covered with blood.

LIBBY. You made a dive at a guy who had a gun?

GILES. I thought they were going to shoot Fred.

(SHE moves to touch him, but HE stands and moves away.)

GILES. Look, don't sentimentalize this! It wasn't a heroic act—just reflexive, so don't exaggerate it into one of your stupid headlines.

LIBBY. I still think—

GILES. I was drunk, for God's sake! I didn't even know what I was doing! *(Unbidden tears spring to his eyes. HE angrily wipes them away.)* Damn! *(HE wipes them again.)* Damn! It seems this is my day to—blub.

(SHE moves to get his cigarettes, lights one, inhales, sees HIM watching her.)

LIBBY. I used to smoke. I gave it up three years, four months, and two days ago. Funny, I don't miss it a bit. *(SHE hands him cigarette.)*

GILES. *(Tears welling up again.)* Oh, hell!

LIBBY. He's going to come through, Giles. I promise.

GILES. I'm not upset—just about Fred—it's me.

LIBBY. You?

(HE moves away to window, his back to her.)

GILES. *(Angrily.)* Look, all my life I've been—careful—never took any chances—played it safe—so—I've never been—tested. Well, today I was. Pathetic. (*HE turns, very vulnerable.*) You're sure he'll be okay?

LIBBY. Sure. I've got those doctors scared shitless.

GILES. I noticed.

LIBBY. Did my yelling offend you?

GILES. No. It just made me feel guilty. Fred is my friend—I was the one who should have been shouting.

LIBBY. I think you did a lot more than shout.

GILES. I should have smashed my fist into their ugly faces!

LIBBY. What did you do when you came to?

GILES. What? Oh, after I saw how badly hurt Fred was, I tried to flag down a taxi, but none of the sons of bitches would stop. So I got him up here.

LIBBY. On your own?

GILES. No, I bribed one of the homeless men into helping.

LIBBY. Bribed?

GILES. I gave him my watch.

LIBBY. (*Peering at him.*) Giles, what's that below your pants cuff?

GILES. What?

LIBBY. My God, it's blood. Pull your pant leg up. (*HE does.*) Why didn't they put something on that at the hospital?

GILES. I didn't even feel it.

LIBBY. Just stand still—I'll get a bandage. (*SHE moves to get a first-aid kit.*)

GILES. Are you sure the hospital has this number?

LIBBY. Positive. Oh, I forgot to tell you. Right before you were mugged someone called for you.

GILES. Who?

LIBBY. Your ex-wife.

GILES. What?

LIBBY. Phillipa. High English voice. Ring a bell?

GILES. (*Carefully*.) Well, I was married to a girl with that name.

LIBBY. (*Dryly*.) Probably the same girl. (*SHE moves to him, tries to lift pant cuff.*)

GILES. How did she know I was in the States?

LIBBY. She said she saw you on that interview on "Entertainment Tonight."

GILES. Yes, she was always attracted to the notorious. Probably why she married me in the first place.

LIBBY. (*Puzzled*.) You weren't famous then, were you?

GILES. My parents were. How did she know where I was staying?

LIBBY. My name was mentioned in the interview, so I guess she must have checked the phone books in L.A. and New York and come up with my number. She obviously went to a *lot* of trouble.

GILES. Probably thinks I'm rolling in money now.

LIBBY. You'd better drop your pants, Giles.

GILES. What?

(*SHE indicates. HE doesn't move.*)

LIBBY. Look, I know you're angry at me, but you don't have to be a friend to apply antiseptic.

(*HE drops his pants to his ankles. SHE starts to swab knee.*)

LIBBY. So about your ex-wife. What's the story?

GILES. Haven't you gathered yet that I don't like discussing my personal life?

LIBBY. Yeah, but I thought you might make an exception with your pants down. What's she doing in Cleveland?

GILES. You never give up, do you? You just keep boring in.

LIBBY. Old habit.

GILES. All right, she married an American.

LIBBY. She left you for an American?

GILES. In a manner of speaking.

LIBBY. What's that mean? She either did or she didn't.

GILES. He bought her.

LIBBY. Bought her what?

GILES. Her. He bought *her*.

LIBBY. You mean, as in "Think I'll go to merry old England and buy me a wife?"

GILES. He had money to burn and, if there was anything she wanted, he just bought it. He was used to just buying things. She was young—and he took advantage of that—and he seduced her with his money. And while he was doing this, I was idiot enough to let him stay in our house. (*HE pulls his pants up, moves away.*)

LIBBY. I'm sorry, Giles.

GILES. Look, I happened to lose my wife to the son of the owner of a chain of appliance stores in Cleveland, but that's not the reason for my antipathy. One doesn't need a personally bad experience to develop an aversion to America!

LIBBY. I understand.

GILES. (*Looks at her.*) That's it? No acid comment? No wisecracks?

LIBBY. There's nothing funny about being abandoned. (*A moment of contact.*) How's your leg?

GILES. Fine, thank you. Didn't the hospital say they'd phone us about Fred's condition?

LIBBY. Try and relax, Giles. Daisy is at the hospital looking out for him, and we have the best health care in the world in New York.

GILES. You need it.

LIBBY. I'm too tired to argue.

GILES. That'll be the day.

(*The door opens and FRED, his head bandaged, and DAISY enter. SHE is looking tense and on edge.*
Instinctively, GILES moves to Fred, puts his hands on his shoulders.)

GILES. Fred, are you all right, old chap?

FRED. Well, it's odd. Usually I'm not too macho about this sort of thing. I mean I have to go to bed for four days after a bad *haircut.* But I never felt better.

DAISY. He's on painkillers.

FRED. Yes, they gave me some—what was that lovely medicine called, love?

DAISY. Darvon.

FRED. Bloody marvelous. Now I know what the expression "feeling no pain" means.

GILES. You think you'll be up to flying today?

FRED. I think I'm flying already.

GILES. Well, luckily they didn't get our passports or airline tickets. This afternoon we'll get out of this hellhole.

FRED. (*Mildly.*) America didn't mug us, Giles. Three hooligans did. Well, it could happen anywhere, couldn't it? I mean no place is perfect, is it? Well, I'm missing my beauty sleep. Think I'll grab some kip.

DAISY. I'll come in and tuck you in.

FRED. Lovely. (*HE exits.*)

GILES. (*Bitterly.*) Yes, well, I don't care what Fred says. That couldn't happen anywhere. It certainly couldn't happen in our village.

LIBBY. But what about a few miles away at one of your soccer games? There's violence on your streets too!

GILES. But at least we're still *shocked* by it! At least —

DAISY. Oh, for God's sake, stop it! Just stop it!!

(THEY stare in amazement at her uncharacteristic outburst.)

LIBBY. Daisy, what—what's the matter with you?

DAISY. (*Hotly.*) I'll tell you what's the matter with me! On the way home we got one of those cab drivers who just *assume* you share all their prejudiced views. Maybe it was my accent that made him free to say anything that came into his head, but this bozo was spilling his guts about the spics, the niggers, the micks and the queers. But finally he runs out of steam and Fred quietly says: "Don't you think we should stop judging people by the way they look or dress?" The guy turns around and says "What you say, Mac?" Fred says "You know, as long as we think people who wear robes or beards or turbans are really different from us, we're going to keep having wars because, if we believe they're not human, it makes it easier to kill them." The driver turns away and I hear him say, under his breath: "Fucking limey." Does that story *mean* anything to you?!

LIBBY. Well, I'm not sure what—

DAISY. This guy is an ignorant slob, but you two should know better!!

GILES. Daisy, I don't think you can compare—

DAISY. You know why people talk like that? So they don't have to get *involved*!!

(There is a tense pause.)

DAISY. *(Finally.)* Look, I'm sorry about losing it like that. It's been a tough night. *(A beat.)* Well, I'm bushed. Think I'll check in on Fred and head for home. *(SHE exits to bedroom.)*

LIBBY. *(Finally.)* We're not like that cab driver, Giles.

GILES. I don't know. She may have a point.

LIBBY. I'd hate to think so.

(A pause.)

GILES. Where are our passports and tickets?

LIBBY. In the coffee table drawer.

(HE moves to get them. SHE watches him.)

LIBBY. Listen, about my behavior in L.A. I was wrong.

(HE looks at her, but doesn't say anything.)

LIBBY. Well, big surprise—I said it without choking or anything. Look, I behaved like a jerk.

GILES. Why?

LIBBY. (*Looks at him for a moment.*) You want the full catastrophe?

GILES. No. I have a plane to catch, so why don't we just "cut to the chase"?

LIBBY. You're still not too crazy about me, are you?

(*HE doesn't answer.*)

LIBBY. That's not a tough question, Giles.

GILES. It is actually.

LIBBY. Okay—I was pretty hot stuff in this business for a while. A real winner. Trouble was, I got so used to winning, I had real trouble with losing.

GILES. Yes, you're the most American person I know.

LIBBY. You mean aggressive—and *please* don't say it's the same thing. I'm not typical. Anyway, I married late and I was determined that would succeed too. Then the marriage started to fall apart—mostly my fault—no, all my fault—I was obsessed with my career, tried to juggle everything— and went out of control. Dan—my husband—got custody of our daughter. I was in no shape to be a parent and—it was her choice. Look, I don't blame her—when you're a teenager, having a drunk for a mother is—well, anyway, by the time I was sober I'd lost her completely.

GILES. She never forgave you?

LIBBY. I saw her last week when we were in L.A. The scars are still there but—maybe someday. And you're thinking "What the hell has this to do with my behavior in a network story conference?" Right?

GILES. No, that's not what I'm thinking.

LIBBY. You see, my fantasy was to do something—succeed at something that would regain her respect. You know, "See, Cindy, I really am a worthwhile person you can be proud of." I thought our project might be it. Stupid—but when it looked as if it might not happen, I got desperate and caved in. I just went a little crazy. I'm sorry.

GILES. Why didn't you tell me?

LIBBY. Because I don't like grovelling—unless it works, of course.

(HE doesn't smile.)

LIBBY. Anyway, I didn't think you were the sort of man to be swayed by sentiment.

GILES. Is that the impression I give?

LIBBY. Until today. That's why I was so happy to see you sobbing uncontrollably earlier.

GILES. I was not "sobbing uncontrollably," and I think it's really bad form for you to bring it up.

LIBBY. What can I tell you? Sometimes I push too hard.

GILES. Yes, well, I appreciate your telling me this. I wouldn't have wanted to leave harboring the ill feeling I had about you. (*HE has found the passports and tickets.*) Ah, here they are.

LIBBY. (*Shaken.*) But you're still leaving?

GILES. (*Looks at her for a moment.*) It's too late for us, Libby.

LIBBY. Oh?

GILES. Let's face it—we're just too—set in our ways; too—too damned old.

LIBBY. We don't have to be.

GILES. (*Dryly.*) It's not something about which one has a choice.

LIBBY. Yes, we do. Nobody gets old just merely by living a number of years.

GILES. (*Sardonically.*) Oh, of course, it's just a state of mind.

LIBBY. It is, in a way.

GILES. That's a sentimental notion.

LIBBY. Of course it is. If you become pessimistic and cynical, then you are old. Giles, we've got to stay curious about the "what next?"

GILES. Maybe there is no "next," Libby.

LIBBY. There can be. Timidity is the enemy. It's really a question of courage.

GILES. To do what?

LIBBY. Take a chance. Keep our appetite for adventure. Not to be so frightened we settle for serenity.

GILES. Why do you think I'm frightened?

LIBBY. Because I am.

GILES. You?

LIBBY. If you tell anyone, I'll deny it.

GILES. What are you frightened of, Libby?

LIBBY. Life. Us.

GILES. Us?

LIBBY. It won't be easy, kid. Living with me is no day at the beach, and you're not exactly the Student Prince at Heidelberg either.

GILES. What are you trying to say, Libby?

LIBBY. That I'd like you to—hang around, of course.

GILES. Why?

LIBBY. Why? My God, does everything have to be stated?

GILES. No, not everything.

LIBBY. Okay, because I could use the company.

GILES. (*Incredulous.*) That's the best reason you can think of for committing to a passionate relationship? *That you can use the company!*

LIBBY. All right! Because I don't want to be lonely for the rest of my life. (*With an effort.*) I don't want to lose you, Giles, so—please—please don't leave. Don't leave me, Giles.

(Very touched by her vulnerability, HE moves to take her face in his hands and tenderly kisses her.)

LIBBY. (*Gently.*) Is that all you think about—sex?

GILES. No, that was offered more in the spirit of— affection.

LIBBY. Does this mean you'll stay?

GILES. I don't know—I need to think it—you see, you're right, I'm terrified. My insides are churning and— I'm not sure I can handle—all this.

LIBBY. Anything I can do to help?

GILES. A good long hug might be—calming.

LIBBY. Easiest thing in the world, but I've been in these clothes for twenty-four hours. It's not good to be old and smell bad too. Why don't I get into something—more appropriate? (*Gently.*) Hold the thought. (*SHE exits to bedroom.*)

(HE moves to deposit his passport as DAISY enters.)

DAISY. You leaving today?

GILES. We have tickets on the afternoon flight.

DAISY. (*Kisses him.*) 'Bye, Giles. I'm sorry we didn't give you a happy ending.

GILES. Well, you know us, we're not too comfortable with happy.

DAISY. (*Smiles, moves to front door, turns.*) Oh, I almost forgot. A guy was waiting in the doorway downstairs. He gave me this for you. (*SHE extracts a paper-wrapped object, gives it to him.*) What is it?

GILES. My watch.

(*SHE exits. HE puts on watch, crosses to look at the two flags in vase, takes them out, one in each hand.*

We hear LOUD ROCK MUSIC from upstairs. HE crosses to get broom to knock on ceiling, but before he does this, the music starts to get to him and HE begins to sway to the beat.

Gradually, it takes him over and he begins to dance, somewhat cautiously at first, but eventually building to a wild, abandoned, totally uninhibited frenzy.

LIBBY, in other clothes, appears in the doorway, stops in complete surprise at what SHE sees, smiles, watches him as, oblivious to her presence, HE moves around the room. HE finally sees her, stops; SHE moves to him, starts to dance. After a moment, HE dances with her.)

GILES. (*Shouting over music.*) I think I'm ready to risk happiness!

LIBBY. Yeah, how come?

GILES. Because I love you.

LIBBY. What?

*(The VOLUME OF THE MUSIC IS REDUCED, but we
still hear it.)*

GILES. (*Still shouting.*) I love you!

*(LIBBY is rendered speechless for a moment before SHE
lapses into an unconscious mimicry of him.)*

LIBBY. Ah.
GILES. (*More quietly.*) I love you.

*(SHE puts her arms around him and they sway to the
MUSIC.)*

GILES. You know, you mustn't expect this sort of
thing to happen every day.
LIBBY. What sort of thing?
GILES. This shouting, crying, and behaving so
emotionally.
LIBBY. Oh, you mean being human.
GILES. Yes. It's just too exhausting.

*(SHE starts to laugh, which builds until her laughter
changes to tears. THEY cling to one another.)*

GILES. Why are you crying?
LIBBY. Because you are.
GILES. You're not so tough.
LIBBY. Don't know what got into me.

(HE wipes her eyes with his thumb through following.)

GILES. You think you could stand to lead an ordered life?

LIBBY. You think you can stand me treading all over your toast?

GILES. I think anything is possible, Libby. I could make some money from the British rights.

LIBBY. *(Teasing.)* But are you willing to spend it?

GILES. Small price to be comfortable in my own skin.

LIBBY. What does that?

GILES. You do.

LIBBY. Is that a definite offer?

GILES. Come live with me, Libby.

LIBBY. At your house?

GILES. Of course.

LIBBY. *(Looks at him for a moment.)* No, my living in England is a deal breaker.

GILES. Well, I'm certainly not living here. How about a compromise? *(Still moving, HE kisses her.)* How about three months here and nine months in England?

LIBBY. Four months there and eight here. *(SHE kisses him.)*

GILES. Look, I'm having trouble concentrating. Could we talk about this later?

(Behind her back his tight grip breaks the stems of the flags; HE drops both of them into the metal wastepaper basket with a CLUNK.)

LIBBY. What was that?

GILES. Our past.

(As THEY sink onto the sofa:)

    LIBBY. Where do we go from here, Giles?
    GILES. *(Looks at her for a moment.)* We create our own country.

(As THEY start to make love, the LIGHTS DIM TO BLACK and the play is over.)

THE END

TWO NEW COMEDIES FROM
SAMUEL FRENCH, Inc.

FAST GIRLS. (Little Theatre). Comedy. Diana Amsterdam. 2m., 3f. Int. Lucy Lewis is a contemporary, single woman in her thirties with what used to be called a "healthy sex life," much to the chagrin of her mother, who feels Lucy is too fast, too easy—and too single. Her best friend, on the other hand, neighbor Abigail McBride, is deeply envious of Lucy's ease with men. When Lucy wants to date a man she just calls him up, whereas Abigail sits home alone waiting for Ernest, who may not even know she exists, to call. The only time Abigail isn't by the phone is after Lucy has had a hot date, when she comes over to Lucy's apartment to hear the juicy details and get green with envy. Sometimes, though, Lucy doesn't want to talk about it, which drives Abigail *nuts* ("If you don't tell me about men I have no love life!"). Lucy's mother arrives to take the bull by the horns, so to speak, arriving with a challenge. Mom claims no man will marry Lucy (even were she to *want to* get married), because she's too easy. Lucy takes up the challenge, announcing that she is going to get stalwart ex-boyfriend Sidney ("we're just friends") Epstein to propose to her. Easier said than done. Sidney doesn't *want* a fast girl. Maybe dear old Mom is right, thinks Lucy. Maybe fast girls *can't* have it all. "Amsterdam makes us laugh, listen and think."—Daily Record. "Brilliantly comic moments."—The Monitor. "rapidly paced comedy with a load of laughs . . . a funny entertainment with some pause for reflection on today's [sexual] confusion."—Suburban News. "Takes a penetrating look at [contemporary sexual chaos]. Passion, celibacy, marriage, fidelity are just some of the subjects that Diana Amsterdam hilariously examines."—Tribune News. **(#8149)**

ADVICE FROM A CATERPILLAR. (Little Theatre.) Comedy. Douglas Carter Beane. 2m. 2f. 1 Unit set & 1 Int. Ally Sheedy and Dennis Christopher starred in the delightful off-Broadway production of this hip new comedy. Ms. Sheedy played Missy, an avant garde video artist who specializes in re-runs of her family's home videos, adding her own disparaging remarks. Needless to say, she is very alienated from the middle-class, family values she grew up with, which makes her very *au courant*, but strangely unhappy. She has a successful career and a satisfactory love-life with a businessman named Suit. Suit's married, but that doesn't stop him and Missy from carrying on. Something's missing, though—and Missy isn't sure what it is, until she meets Brat. He is a handsome young aspiring actor. Unfortunately, Brat is also the boyfriend of Missy's best friend. Sound familiar? It isn't—because Missy's best friend is a gay man named Spaz! Spaz has been urging Missy to find an unmarried boyfriend, but this is too much—too much for Spaz, too much for Suit and, possibly, too much for Missy. Does she *want* a serious relationship (ugh—how bourgeois!)? Can a bisexual unemployed actor actually be her Mr. Wonderful? "Very funny … a delightful evening."—Town & Village. **(#3876)**

OTHER PUBLICATIONS FOR YOUR INTEREST

MIXED FEELINGS
(Little Theatre—Comedy)

Donald Churchill
m., 2 f., Int.

This is a riotous comedy about divorce, that ubiquitous, peculiar institution which so shapes practically everyone's life. Arthur and Norma, ex-spouses, live in separate apartments in the same building. Norma has second thoughts about her on-going affair with Arthur's best-friend; while Arthur isn't so sure he wants to continue *his* dalliance with Sonia, wife of a manufacturer with amusingly kinky sexual tastes (Dennis—the manufacturer—doesn't mind that his wife is having an affair; just so long as she continues to provide him with titillating accounts of it while he is dressed as a lady traffic cop). Most of Sonia's accounts are pure fiction, which seems to keep Dennis happy. Comic sparks are ignited into full-fledged farcical flames in the second act, when Dennis arrives in Arthur's flat for lessons in love from the legendary Arthur! "Riotous! A domestic laught romp! A super play. You'll laugh all the way home, I promise you.'—Eastbourne News. "Very funny ... a Churchill comedy that most people will thoroughly enjoy."—The Stage. Restricted New York City.

THE DECORATOR
(Little Theatre/Comedy)

Donald Churchill
m., 2 f., Int.

Much to her surprise, Marcia returns home to find that her flat has not been painted, as she arranged. In fact, the job hasn't even been started yet. There on the premises is the housepainter who is filling in for his ill colleague. As he begins work, there is a surprise visitor--the wife of the man with whom Marcia is having an affair, who has come to confront her nemesis and to exact her revenge by informing Marcia's husband of his wife's infidelity. Marcia is at her wit's end about what to do, until she gets a brilliant idea. It seems the housepainter is a part-time professional actor. Marcia hires him to impersonate her husband, Reggie, at the big confrontation later that day, when the wronged wife plans to return and spill the beans. Hilarity is piled upon hilarity as the housepainter, who takes his acting *very* seriously, portrays the absent Reggie. The wronged wife decides that the best way to get back at Marcia would be to sleep with her "husband" (the house painter), which is an ecstatic experience for them both. When Marcia learns that the housepainter/actor/husband has slept with her rival, she demands to have the opportunity to show the housepainter what *really* good sex is. "This has been the most amazing day of my life", says the sturdy painter, as Marcia leads him into her bedroom. "Irresistible."—London Daily Telegraph.